KNOTS

STEP BY STEP

KNOTS
STEP BY STEP

DES PAWSON

**LONDON, NEW YORK
MUNICH, MELBOURNE,
AND DELHI**

Project Editor Ed Wilson
Project Art Editor Keith Davis
Production Editor Ben Marcus
Production Controller
Mandy Inness
Jacket Designer Silke Spingies
Managing Editor
Stephanie Farrow
Managing Art Editor Lee Griffiths

Photography Sam Scott-Hunter

DK INDIA
Senior Editor Nidhi Sharma
Editor Pallavi Singh
Designers Simran Kaur, Vikas
Sachdeva, Kanika Mittal
DTP Designer Shanker Prasad
DTP Manager Balwant Singh
Managing Art Editor
Romi Chakraborty
Managing Editor Saloni Talwar

First published in
Great Britain
in 2012 by
Dorling Kindersley Limited

Penguin Group (UK)
4 6 8 10 9 7 5
010 – 183048 – April / 2012

A CIP catalogue record for
this book is available from
the British Library.

ISBN 978-1-4093-8317-8

Colour reproduction by
Scanhouse, Malaysia.
Printed and bound in China by
Leo Paper Products, Ltd.
Discover more at **www.dk.com**

Contents

BENDS

Sheet Bend
Tucked Sheet Bend
Double Sheet Bend
Rope Yarn Knot
Carrick Bend
Hunter's Bend
Lanyard Knot
Ashley's Bend
Fisherman's Knot
Double Fisherman's Knot
Best for... Climbing
Blood Knot
Water Knot

HITCHES

Rolling Hitch
Mirrored Rolling Hitch
Round Turn & Two
　　Half Hitches
Buntline Hitch
Fisherman's Bend
Best for... Camping
Cow Hitch
Pedigree Cow Hitch
Cow Hitch with Toggle
Sheepshank
Sheepshank Man o' War
Marlinespike Hitch
Highwayman's Hitch
Waggoner's Hitch
Snelling a Hook
Clinch Knot
Improved Clinch Knot
Palomar Knot
Square Lashing
Diagonal Lashing
Best for... Gardening
Sheer Lashing
Icicle Hitch
Prusik Knot
Bachmann Knot
Klemheist Knot
Italian Hitch
Reversed Italian Hitch

LOOPS

Alpine Butterfly
Bowline
Bowline – Second Method
Bowline with Two Turns

PLAITS & SENNITS

SPLICES & WHIPPINGS

Introduction

Knots have been used throughout history, and they remain a valuable resource today. Learning to tie knots is a handy, enjoyable skill, requiring only simple equipment to get started.

This book contains a selection of knots intended to be practical and instructive. Many of them have specific purposes, others are purely decorative, while some can be used for many different tasks; all of them should be reliable and safe if tied correctly. You will find them useful in everyday life as well as in activities such as climbing, sailing, and camping.

As with any skill, it is best to begin by learning the basics. Familiarize yourself with the fundamental techniques, the different types of rope and their uses, and a few technical terms. Use the rope attached to this book to experiment with some simple knots before you attempt anything complicated; classic knots such as the Reef Knot (*see pp.85–86*) and the Overhand Knot (*see pp.28–29*) are both excellent places to begin.

When learning to tie new knots, don't rush – pause regularly to make adjustments as needed and above all, have fun!

bout this Book

ead the brief description at the start of each chapter to
ork out which type of knot you need, then use the icons
d text at the beginning of each knot to refine your search.
nce you have found the knot you are looking for, follow
e step-by-step instructions to learn how it is tied. This
ook also contains information on rope and tools, and
e best knots for activities such as sailing and climbing.

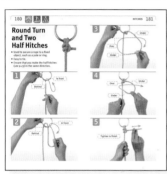

**Step-by-step
knot sequence**
Opening with an
overview of the function
and characteristics
of the knot, these
pages use step-by-step
photography,
accompanied by
clear instructions,
to demonstrate how
the knot is tied.

**Getting
started**
This section
outlines the
equipment
and basic
techniques
needed to tie
the knots
featured in
this book.

Best for...
These
feature
pages profile
the six best
knots for
specific
activities
such as
gardening
or fishing.

cons

he activities for which each knot can be used are indicated
y these icons:

 General   **Fishing**   **Climbing**

 Sailing   **Camping**   **Decorative**

Getting Started

Using the correct type of rope for a particular task is key to tying knots effectively. This chapter details how the properties of rope vary according to its construction and composition, with useful advice on storage and maintenance and a range of basic terms and techniques.

Rope Construction

The rope-making process involves fibre being spun into yarn. The yarn is then twisted into large strands or braided, sometimes around a core. The qualities of a rope are partly determined by this process.

Three-strand rope

Rope with three strands is made by twisting fibres into yarns, then twisting the yarns together into strands. Three of the strands are then twisted into rope. At each stage the direction of the twist is opposite to that of the stage before: this creates the friction that holds all the strands together.

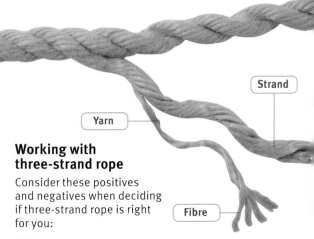

Strand

Yarn

Fibre

Working with three-strand rope

Consider these positives and negatives when deciding if three-strand rope is right for you:

✓ Firm and flexible.

✓ Easy to splice (*see pp.334–63*).

✓ Perfect for rigging traditional sailing vessels.

✓ A good choice for decorative knotting.

✗ Strands will untwist unless the ends are whipped (*see p.14*) to stop them from fraying.

✗ Kinks easily while being coiled.

✗ May have too much stretch for some tasks

aided rope

e most common type of this rope has a braided cover
h a core of woven or twisted yarn made from synthetic
res. The fibres in the core and the cover are not always
same. Many braided ropes are developed for
ecialized purposes.

Cover

Core

rking with
aided rope

nsider these positives and
gatives when deciding if
ided rope is right for you:

Has a smooth feel
and good flexibility.

Suitable for a variety
of purposes.

✓ Has less stretch and
less tendency to kink
than three-strand rope.

✓ Reliable in situations
where safety is
paramount, such as
mountaineering and
climbing.

✗ Difficult to splice.
Some braided rope
cannot be spliced at all.

Fishing Line

- Fishing line is usually thin
and slippery – you may need
to use special knots, often
with many turns (*see p.17*),
when working with it.

To help bed the turns into
place, moisten the line prior to
working it tight. This will make
the knot difficult to untie.

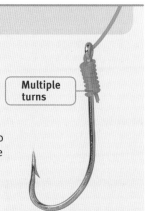

Multiple
turns

Rope Materials

Until the second half of the 20th century all rope was made from natural plant fibres. Since then, however, synthetic fibres have taken over, and now most rope is manufactured from synthetic materials.

Natural rope

The most common natural fibres in use today are cotton, sisal, and manila. They are aesthetically pleasing but tend to decay quickly and wear out faster than synthetic fibres.

Cotton

Fibres of cotton grow around the seeds of the plant. They can be used to make soft, smooth ropes.

- Stretchy and soft to touch.

- Used mainly for decorative purposes.

- Commonly used for animal halters.

Sisal

Fibres of sisal are stiff and come from the agave plant.

- Inexpensive and fairly coarse.

- Holds knots well.

- Can be treated with a waterproofing agent, making it suitable for exposure to moisture.

Manila

Fibres of manila come from the abaca plant.

- One of the strongest natural ropes.

- Less susceptible to decay than sisal and cotton.

Synthetic rope

Synthetic fibres are stronger than natural fibres and are resistant to decay. The most common synthetics used for making rope are polypropylene, polyester, and nylon.

Polypropylene

Polypropylene is low-cost and varied in form.

Has a tendency to break down in sunlight – needs to be treated against ultraviolet rays.

More liable to chafe than other synthetic fibres.

■ Floats in water.

■ Slightly slippery – needs to be tied with a secure knot.

Polyester

Polyester is one of the best ropes for outdoor use.

Wears well – resistant to chafing and sunlight.

As strong as nylon but has less stretch.

■ Can be purchased pre-stretched, meaning there will be minimal stretch during use.

Nylon

Nylon fibres were the first synthetic material to be used for making rope.

Has a degree of stretch particularly good for absorbing shock loads.

Good for making ropes used for mooring boats and climbing.

■ Tends to stiffen over time.

■ Resists the ultraviolet rays in sunlight better than polypropylene, but not as well as polyester.

Rope Maintenance

Good rope maintenance will preserve the strength of a rope and increase its life span. If the rope is being used for activities that carry an element of risk, such as climbing or abseiling, rope maintenance is an essential safety procedure.

Binding ends

Unless they are bound in a process called whipping, the ends of three-strand and braided rope will unravel and fray. The ends of a rope can be finished with either a temporary whipping or a permanent twine whipping.

Permanent whipping

Bear in mind the following points when making a permanent whipping:

- Whipping should be at least one and a half times the diameter of the rope.

Whipping twine

- A Common Whipping (*see pp.374–75*) is quick to make and suitable for three-strand and braided rope.

- The Sailmaker's Whipping (*see pp.379–82*) is suitable for three-strand rope.

- For braided rope, a Palm and Needle Whipping (*see pp.383–86*) is used to bind the core and cover together.

Temporary whipping

If there is not enough time to make a permanent whipping, a temporary whipping can be used. The following methods are all suitable for making a temporary whipping:

Self-adhesive tape

- Self-adhesive tape wrapped around the rope.

- A Constrictor Knot (*see pp.109–10*) tied with thin twine.

- A small amount of quick-drying glue applied to the end of the rope.

- Melting the end of synthetic rope. Be careful to avoid burning your fingers.

ope care

es should be kept free from wear and tear, such as
fing caused by constant rubbing of the fibres against
d or rough surfaces.

oking after rope

following tips will help
to keep your rope in
d condition:

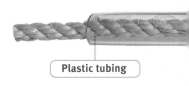

Plastic tubing

o prevent chafing, fix
ne plastic tubing (see
ht) over parts of the rope
t are in constant contact
h a rough surface.

● If the rope does become
worn, avoid putting it under
any strain.

● Clean dirty rope with a
scrubbing brush (see left),
using water and washing-up
liquid. Afterwards, coil the
rope (see pp.16–17) and
hang it up to dry.

Brush the rope

● Rope made from natural
fibres should never be stored
when it is wet because it will
quickly decay.

Rope deterioration

● Worn or broken yarns or fibres sticking
out from a rope are signs of
deterioration.

Untwist the lay of the rope to see if grit
or sand are causing hidden damage.

● Rope that shows signs of deterioration
should not be used for any tasks or
activities that may involve risk to a
person or property.

Worn yarns

Storing Rope

When you are not working with your rope, coil it up neat
to prevent it from becoming tangled and then hang it in
dry place. Make sure natural-fibre rope is completely dr
before you store it away.

Coiling rope

Coil rope carefully into loops with even turns that
follow the twists of the rope's construction. Use
some thin line to hold the loops together so the
coiling cannot be disturbed.

Braided rope

Coil braided rope into figure-
of-eight loops to balance the
left- and right-hand twists
of its strands.

Three-strand rope

Coil three-strand rope
into loops in a clockwise
direction.

Clockwise loops

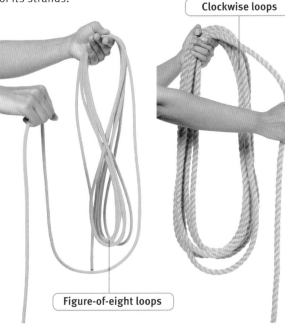

Figure-of-eight loops

aking a self-stopped coil

working end of a rope can be used to
ke a stopper that holds the coils
ether. The stopper can then be
d to hang up the rope.

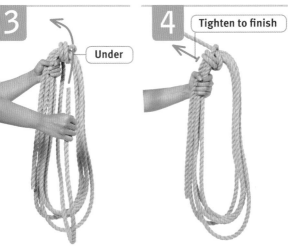

Terms and Tools

To tie the knots in this book, all you need to know are a few important terms, and how to use certain specialist tools that will help you with some of the more complex tasks.

Ends of the rope

The end of the rope that you actively use to make a knot is called the working end. The other end is inactive and is known as the standing part.

Working end

Standing part

Shaping the rope

You can bend a rope into shapes such as a bight, loop, an crossing turn, to help create different knots.

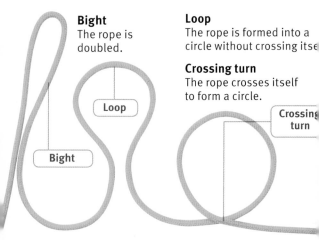

Bight
The rope is doubled.

Loop
The rope is formed into a circle without crossing itse

Crossing turn
The rope crosses itself to form a circle.

Loop

Crossing turn

Bight

ırns around an object

█en you pass the working end of a rope around another
█e, or around an object, the manoeuvre is described
█ making a turn.

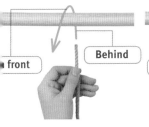

| front | **Behind** |

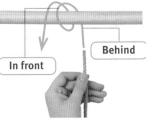

| **In front** | **Behind** |

▌rn

▌urn is a single pass of the
█e around an object. It is
▌o known as a single turn.

Round turn

A round turn is two turns,
or passing the rope twice,
around the object.

▌seful tools

█ew simple but specialized tools will help to make
█rking with rope considerably easier. These tools
█ available from chandlery stores or on the Internet.

Sailmaker's palm and needle
A reinforced glove
and heavy needle.
The glove makes it
easier to push the
needle through
thick rope.

Adhesive tape
For quick,
temporary
whippings.

Sharp knife
Essential for
cutting or
trimming
rope.

Swedish fid
The hollow
blade makes it
easier to tuck
rope when
splicing.

Marlinespike
An all-metal
tool used for
separating
the strands
of a knot.

Netting needle
For working
with thin
line when
making nets.

Techniques

Some basic knot-tying techniques will provide you with the fundamental skills to make both simple and complicated knots in a quick and easy fashion.

Estimating rope length

To estimate how much rope is needed for a knot make a dummy with loose turns, leaving out the actual tucks. It is better to over-estimate how much rope is required rather than run out of cord.

Loose turns

Working with a long length of rope

More complex knots will require a long length of rope. Rather than attempting to manipulate an unwieldy working end, simply form a bight (*see p.18*).

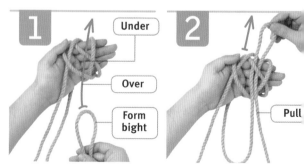

1   **Under**   **Over**   **Form bight**

2   **Pull**

Form the working end into a bight by folding it back on itself before tucking.

After tucking the bight, pull the rest of the working end through.

nlaying and laying rope

me knots and most splices (*see pp.334–63*) are made
h the strands of the rope, rather than the whole rope.
ı can unlay these by opening them up or lay them to
nake the rope.

Unlaying a rope

Tape the end of
each strand as
you unlay it,
making sure you
keep the twist in
the strand intact.

Taped end

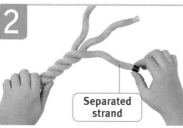

Separate the
strands by gently
untwisting each
one from the body
of the rope.

Separated strand

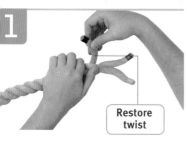

Laying a rope

When relaying an
unlaid piece of
rope, try to restore
the original twist
in each strand
to hold them
together.

Restore twist

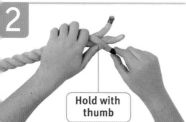

Force the strand
into place with
your thumb before
moving on to the
next strand.

Hold with thumb

Working out the slack

Once you have formed a knot you can systematically work out any slack to make it tighter. Do this a little at a time rather than trying to tighten the whole knot at once.

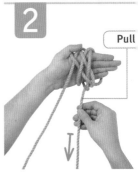

Find a part of the knot that contains slack and pull the slack through.

Work the slack through the knot to the end of the rope.

Tightening a knot

To tighten a knot, pull each end gently and carefully. Try to be systematic when tightening multi-strand knots – an even knot can only be created if all the strands are equally tight

Firmly hold one end of a strand between finger and thumb.

Feel the knot tighten as you pull the end gently through. Repeat with the other strand

rming a half hitch

alf hitch is a simple manoeuvre that is one of the building
cks of knot tying. Usually, half hitches are made around
bject, such as a pole, or another rope.

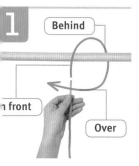 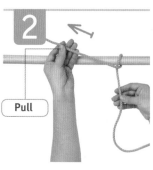

ke a half hitch by taking
rope once around the
ect you are securing it to.

Lock the half hitch in place
by passing one end of the
rope across the other end.

rming a crossing turn

ossing turn, like a half hitch, is the basis of many knots.
an be formed by rolling the rope between the finger and
mb of one hand so that it twists over or under itself to
n a loop.

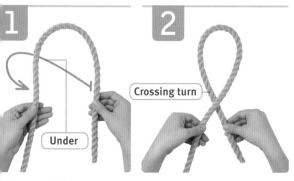

the part of the rope that
lie under the turn
ween the thumb and
ers.

The rope will twist under
itself to form the crossing
turn.

Doubling up

Knots can often be doubled – or even tripled – by replicating the original pattern with additional strands. These should follow the path of the first strand without crossing it.

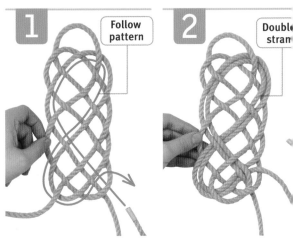

Follow pattern

Double strand

Create the first pattern of the knot, making sure there is enough space for the second pass. Follow around with the second strand.

Ensure that the doubling strand does not cross the original strand. Some knots can be tripled or even quadrupled.

Trimming the ends

Trim ends

When you have finished a knot, a splice, or a whipping, you will probably have some loose ends. Cut off these surplus ends with a sharp knife.

Not too close

Do not trim an end too close to the body of the knot or the splice, as it may pull out when put under strain.

orking into shape

 not will probably need to be coaxed into a neat and
 en shape. This process is known as dressing a knot.
 not that is tidy is likely to be stronger and more secure.

**Arrange
strands**

**Knot
structure**

 orking with your fingers
 d thumbs, push and pull
 strands into shape.
 rns may need to be
 isted tight.

Ensure the strands of the
rope sit neatly alongside
each other, emphasizing
the knot's structure and
increasing effectiveness.

eizing

 izing involves using small line to bind
 gether two parts of a larger rope or two
 more larger ropes positioned side by
 e. Historically, the fixed rigging on
 iling ships were seized rather than
 otted or spliced together.

Seizing

Stopper Knots

Stopper knots are used to stop a rope fraying or unravelling, or to prevent it from being pulled through a hole or block. Some stopper knots are tied with just the strands of the rope, but most are tied with the whole rope.

Overhand Knot

- The simplest of all knots.
- The basis of knots in the bend and loop families.
- Difficult to untie when tightened.
- Also known as the Thumb Knot.

1

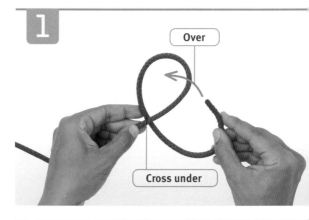

Over

Cross under

2

Under

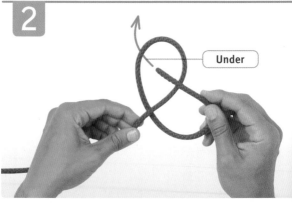

3

Push

4

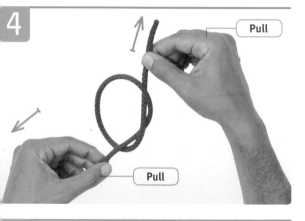

Pull

Pull

5

Tighten to finish

Slipped Overhand Knot

- A simple slipknot that can be tied in the middle or at the end of the rope.
- Easier to untie than the Overhand Knot (*see pp.28–29*).
- Untie by pulling on the short end of the loop.

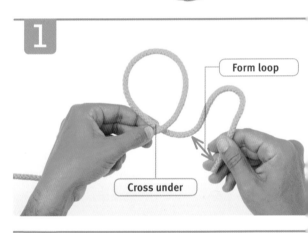

1

Form loop

Cross under

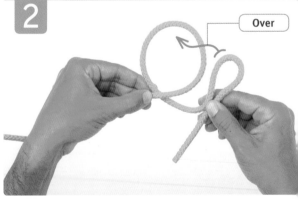

2

Over

3

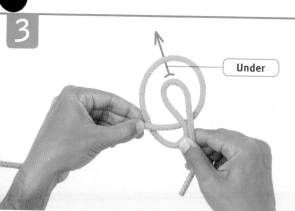

Under

4

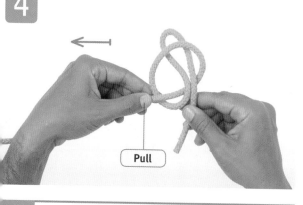

Pull

5

Tighten to finish

Double Overhand Knot

- A secure stopper knot that is difficult to untie.
- Bulkier than the Overhand Knot (*see pp.28–29*).
- Can be made larger by adding extra turns.

1

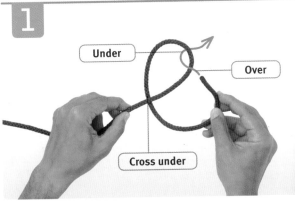

Under

Over

Cross under

2

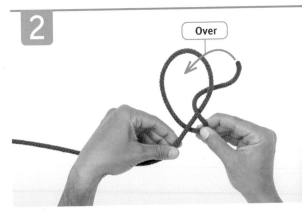

Over

3

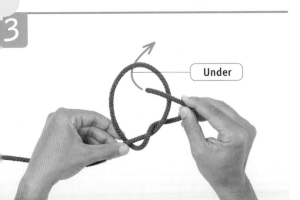

Under

4

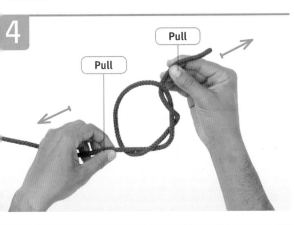

Pull

Pull

5

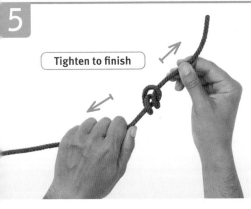

Tighten to finish

EST FOR ...
Sailing

good sailor only needs to know how to tie half a dozen sic knots. These knots will help to secure and control e lines, halyards, lanyards, painters, and sheets on chts, dinghies, and other boats.

owline » pp.240–41

A versatile knot – the Bowline is often called e king of all loop knots.

Easy to tie and untie, so is ideal for tying nyards to fenders, eets to sails, and aking a loop to row over a bollard.

Difficult to untie under strain and can loosen en not under load.

Similar knots:
» pp.246–47
Bowline with Two Turns
» p.248 **Bowline with Stopper**

igure of Eight
pp.38–39

A stopper knot with some bulk that is quick to tie.

Ideal for stopping the end of a rope from nning out through a block.

An easy knot to untie, even if it has been der a lot of strain.

Similar knots:
» pp.44–46
Sink Stopper Knot
» pp.47–48
Stevedore Knot

Sheet Bend » pp.140–41

✓ A quick and easy method of joining two ropes together.

✓ A Double Sheet Bend can be used to tie ropes of different diameters together securely.

✗ Not suitable for joining ropes of different sizes.

Similar knots
» pp.142–43
Tucked Sheet
Bend
» pp.144–45
Double Sheet
Bend

Round Turn and Two Half Hitches » pp.180–81

✓ Perfect for tying a rope to a mooring post or ring, as the round turn takes much of the strain off the rope.

✓ Can be untied easily, even when it is under strain.

✓ The pull of the rope can be at right angles to the ring or post to which it is attached.

Similar knots:
» pp.184–85
Fisherman's Bend

Rolling Hitch
» pp.176–77

✓ Can be used to tie a second line to a sheet in order to relieve strain.

✓ Useful for tying a fender lanyard to a rail.

✗ Can fail if the pull of the lines are not properly aligned.

Similar knots:
» pp.178–79
Mirrored Rolling Hitch

Reef Knot » pp.85–86

✓ Ideal for tying up a bundle of material.

✓ Can also be used to fasten the unused part of a sail around the mast.

✓ Can be slipped for quick release.

✗ Not suitable for joining two ropes together – it may collapse and come undone.

Similar knots:
» pp.87–88
Slipped Reef Knot
» pp.96–98
Surgeon's Knot

Figure of Eight

- Used to prevent a rope from slipping through a hole.
- This knot structure is the basis for several other knots such as the Packer's Knot (*see pp.102–04*).
- Can be tied quickly and untied easily.
- Works well as the base of a loop knot.

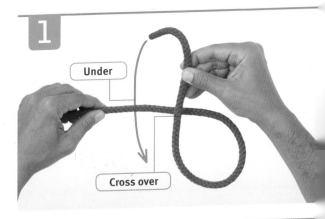

1

Under

Cross over

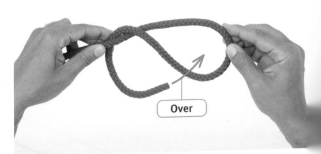

2

Over

3

Under

4

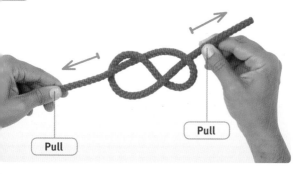

Pull

Pull

5

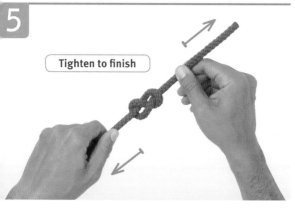

Tighten to finish

Slipped Figure of Eight

- A stopper knot that is quick to tie.
- Easier to untie than the Figure of Eight (see pp.38–39).
- Ensure that you work the knot tight so it does not come undone inadvertently.

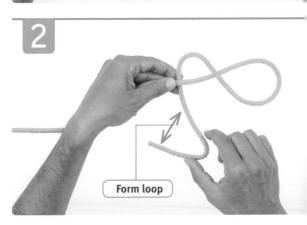

1

Under

Cross over

2

Form loop

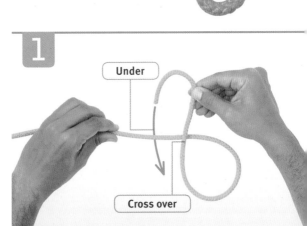

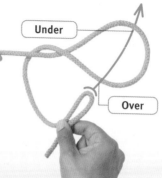

3

Under

Over

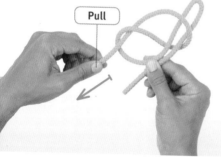

4

Pull

5

Tighten to finish

Stopper Knot

- Gives weight to the end of a rope that needs to be thrown.
- A variation of the Overhand Knot (*see pp.28–29*) and one of the most decorative stopper knots.

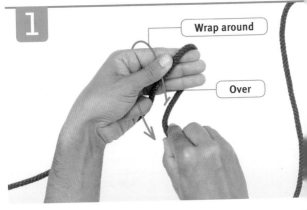

1

Wrap around

Over

2

Wrap around at least four times

Over

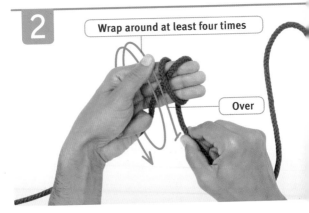

3

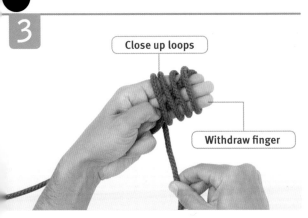

Close up loops

Withdraw finger

4

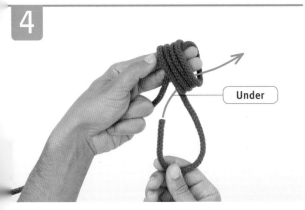

Under

5

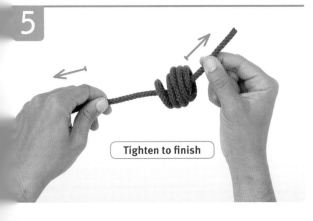

Tighten to finish

Sink Stopper Knot

- Used to prevent a thin rope from slipping through a large hole.
- Needs to be carefully tightened and worked into shape.
- Difficult to untie when tightened.

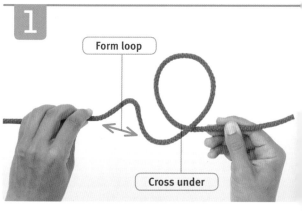

1

Form loop

Cross under

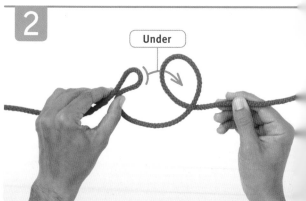

2

Under

3

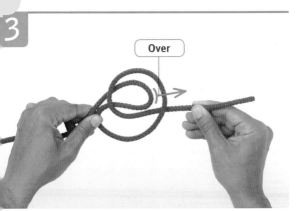

Over

4

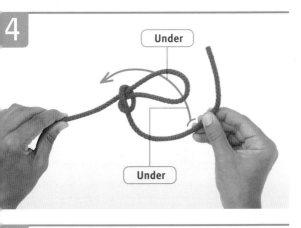

Under

Under

5

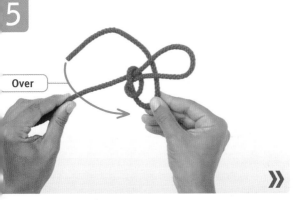

Over

»

6

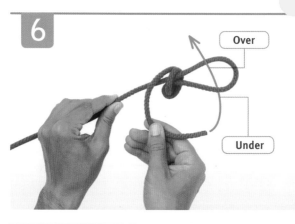

Over

Under

7

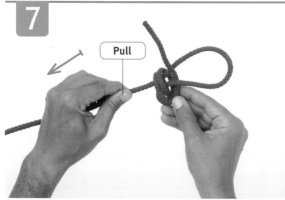

Pull

8

Tighten to finish

Stevedore Knot

Good for preventing a line from slipping.
Starts like the Figure of Eight
(*see pp.38–39*), but its extra turn
forms a bulkier knot that is less
prone to jamming and easier to untie.
Preferred by stevedores or dockworkers.

1

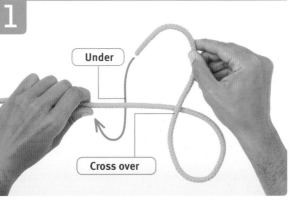

Under

Cross over

2

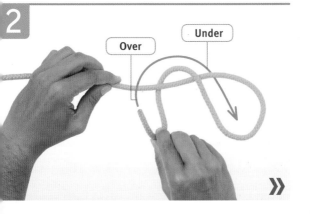

Over

Under

»

3

Over

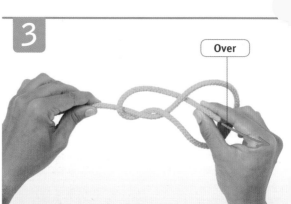

4

Pull

5

Tighten to finish

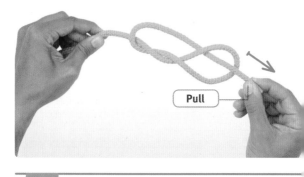
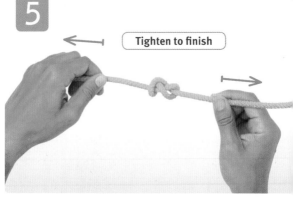

onkey's Fist

lds extra weight to the end of
line that needs to be thrown.

hen working the knot into
ape, ensure that all turns
e even.

hen being used for decorative
rposes, such as a key fob,
ace a wooden ball in the
ntre to add weight.

1

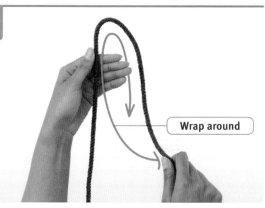

Wrap around

2

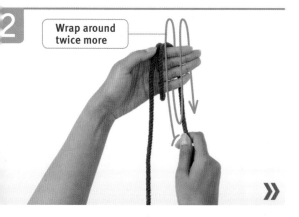

Wrap around
twice more

»

3

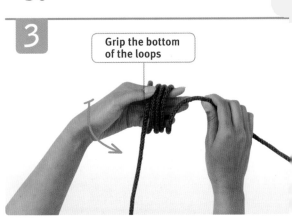

Grip the bottom of the loops

4

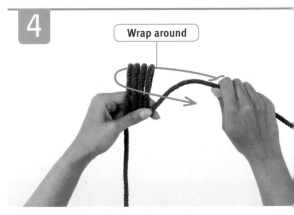

Wrap around

5

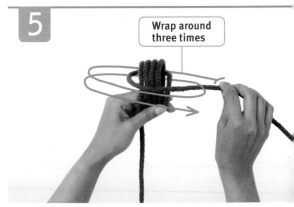

Wrap around three times

6

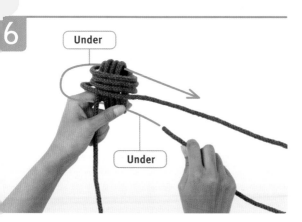

Under

Under

7

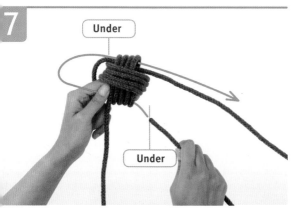

Under

Under

8

Place wooden ball in centre of knot

»

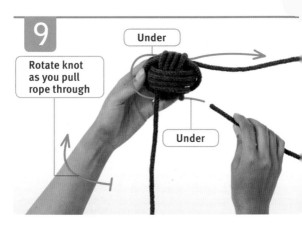

9

Under

Rotate knot as you pull rope through

Under

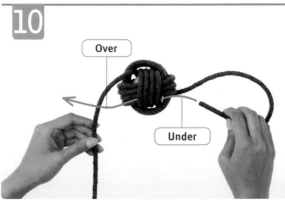

10

Over

Under

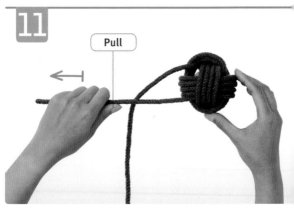

11

Pull

12

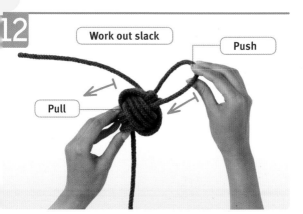

Work out slack

Push

Pull

13

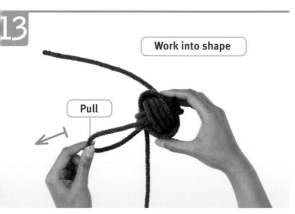

Work into shape

Pull

14

Trim and tuck to finish

Crown Knot

- Used to prevent the ends of a three-strand rope from unravelling.
- Forms the basis of other decorative stoppers such as the Manrope Knot (*see pp.61–71*).
- Ensure that strand ends point downwards.

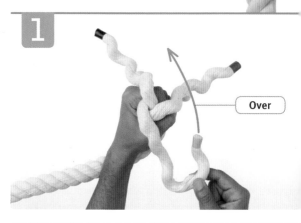

1

Over

2

Over

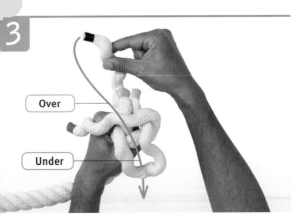

3

Over

Under

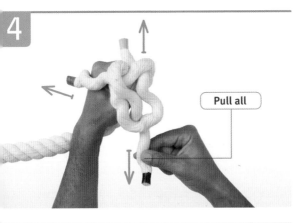

4

Pull all

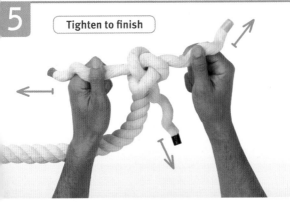

5

Tighten to finish

Wall Knot

- Used in combination with the Crown Knot (see pp.54–55) to make other decorative stopper knots such as the Manrope Knot (see pp.61–71).
- Whip (see pp.374–75) the ends before using as a stopper knot.
- Ensure the ends point upwards from the knot.
- Forms the basis of the Matthew Walker Knot (see pp.58–60).

1 UNLAY STRANDS AT THE END OF A ROPE (>>p.21)

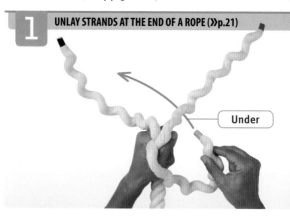

Under

2

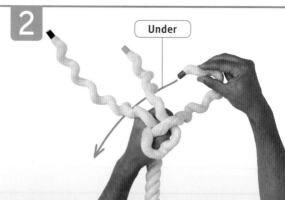

Under

3

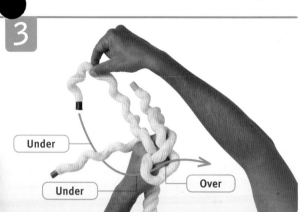

Under

Under

Over

4

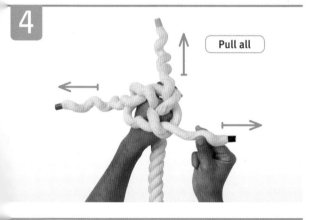

Pull all

5

Tighten to finish

Matthew Walker Knot

- A stopper knot for three-strand rope.
- Can also be made with four strands.
- Traditionally tied at the end of a rope used as a handle for a wooden bucket.

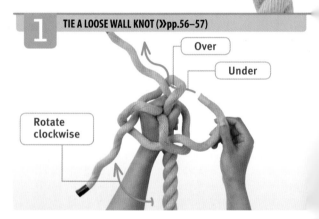

1 TIE A LOOSE WALL KNOT (>>pp.56–57)

Over

Under

Rotate clockwise

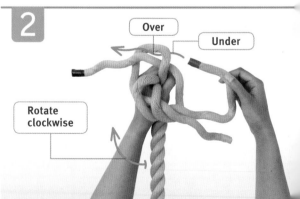

2

Over

Under

Rotate clockwise

3

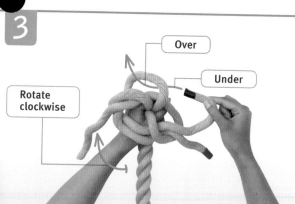

Over

Under

Rotate clockwise

4

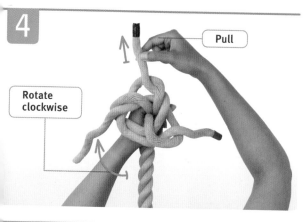

Pull

Rotate clockwise

5

Make a second cycle of tucks

»

6

Pull all

7

Pull all

8

Tighten to finish

anrope Knot

A decorative stopper knot made
by tying a Crown Knot (*see pp.54–55*)
on top of a Wall Knot (*see pp.56–57*).
Traditionally tied on the ends of handrail
ropes used when boarding ships.
Can be doubled but care must be
taken that each strand is positioned
on the same side as the previous one.

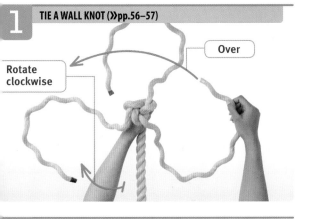

1 | **TIE A WALL KNOT (»pp.56–57)**

Over

Rotate
clockwise

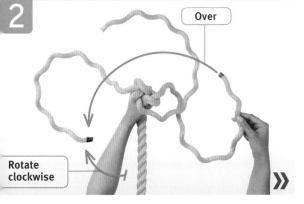

2

Over

Rotate
clockwise

»

3

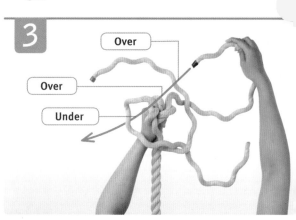

Over

Over

Under

4

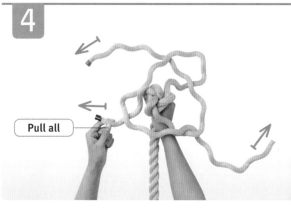

Pull all

5

Locate first
strand end

6

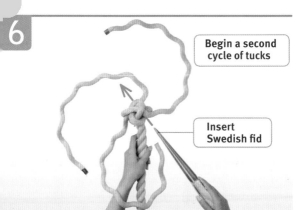

Begin a second cycle of tucks

Insert Swedish fid

7

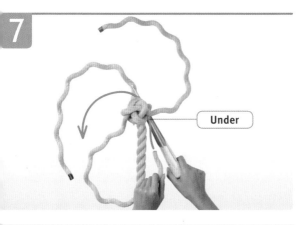

Under

8

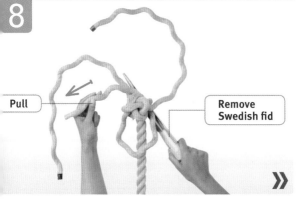

Pull

Remove Swedish fid

»

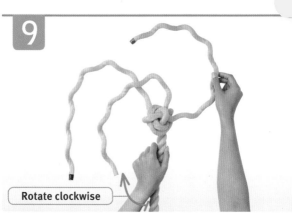

9

Rotate clockwise

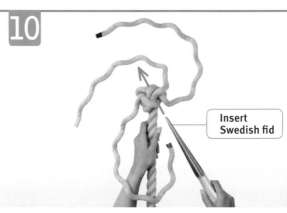

10

Insert
Swedish fid

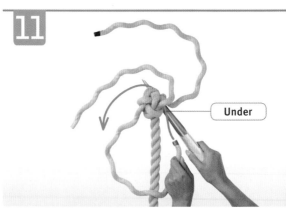

11

Under

12

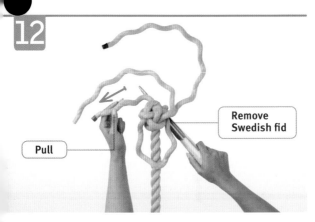

Remove Swedish fid

Pull

13

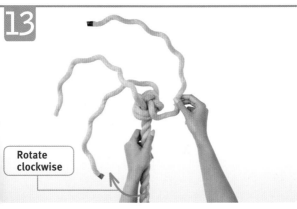

Rotate clockwise

14

Insert Swedish fid

»

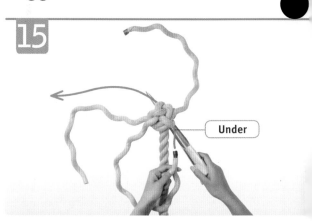

15

Under

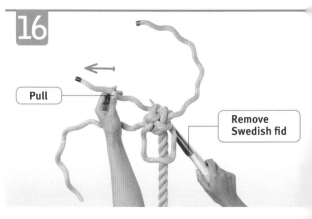

16

Pull

Remove Swedish fid

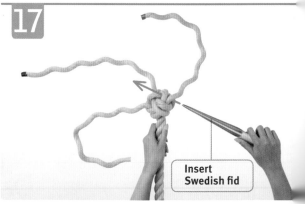

17

Insert Swedish fid

18

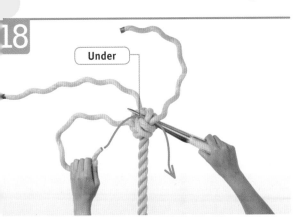

Under

19

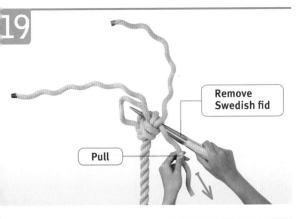

Remove
Swedish fid

Pull

20

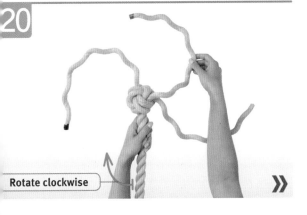

Rotate clockwise

»

21

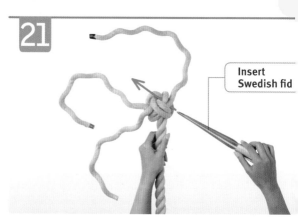

Insert
Swedish fid

22

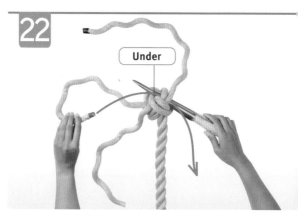

Under

23

Remove
Swedish fid

Pull

24

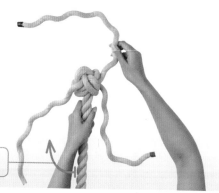

Rotate clockwise

25

Insert Swedish fid

26

Under

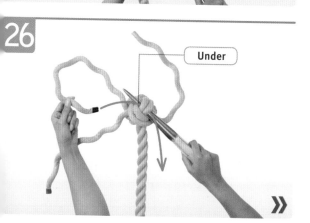

»

27

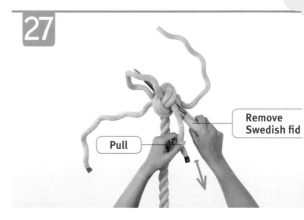

Remove
Swedish fid

Pull

28

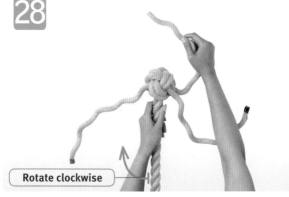

Rotate clockwise

29

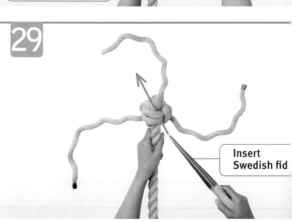

Insert
Swedish fid

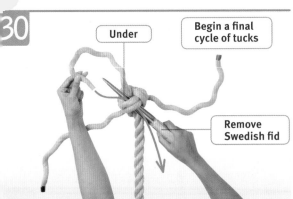

30

Under

Begin a final cycle of tucks

Remove Swedish fid

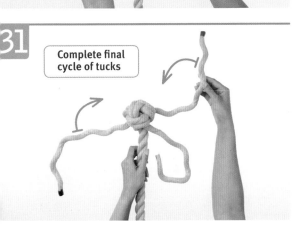

31

Complete final cycle of tucks

32

Tighten to finish

Diamond Knot

- A firm stopper knot tied in the strands of the rope.
- Made by tying a Wall Knot (*see pp.56–57*) below a Crown Knot (*see pp.54–55*).
- Sometimes used as an alternative to the Matthew Walker Knot (*see pp.58–60*).
- To make it easier to thread the strands, use a fid or Swedish fid (*see p.19*).

1 TIE A CROWN KNOT (»pp.54–55)

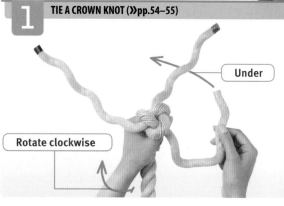

Under

Rotate clockwise

2

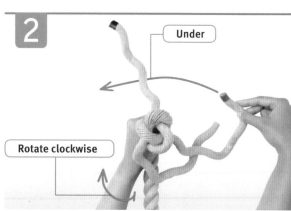

Under

Rotate clockwise

3

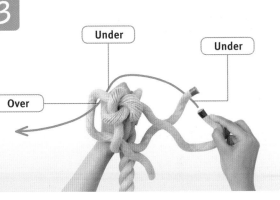

4

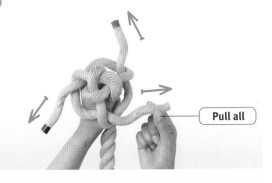

5

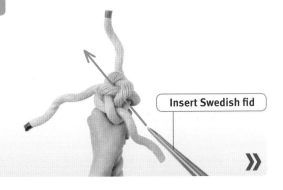

6

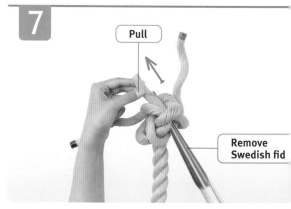

Under

7

Pull

Remove
Swedish fid

8

Arrange strand

9

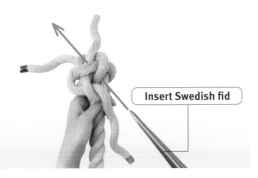

Insert Swedish fid

10

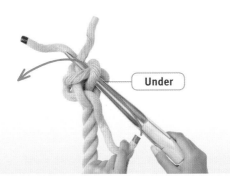

Under

11

Pull

Remove
Swedish fid

»

12

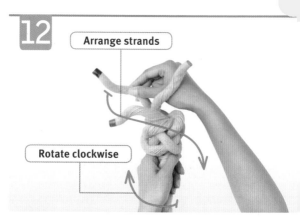

Arrange strands

Rotate clockwise

13

Insert Swedish fid

14

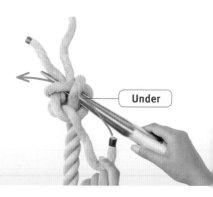

Under

15

Pull

Remove Swedish fid

16

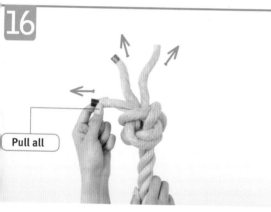

Pull all

17

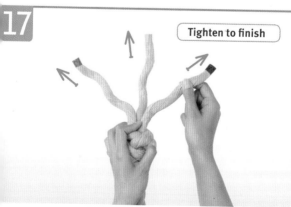

Tighten to finish

Binding Knots

Binding knots can be used to gather in sails, or to bind together a number of loose items such as timbers. They can also be used to tie a rope neatly around an object – for example, to wrap a gift.

True Lover's Knot

- A knot that symbolizes two people joined in love, sometimes found on a ring.
- Links two pieces of rope using interlocking Overhand Knots (see pp.28–29).
- The Overhand Knots should mirror each other perfectly.

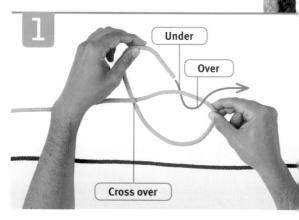

1

Under

Over

Cross over

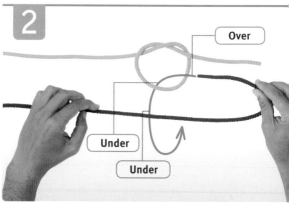

2

Over

Under

Under

3

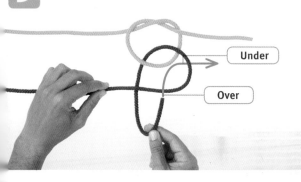

Under

Over

4

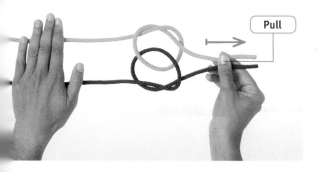

Pull

5

Tighten to finish

Sailor's Cross

- A decorative knot that symbolizes good luck.
- Developed from the True Lover's Knot (*see pp.80–81*).

1

Cross under

Over

Under

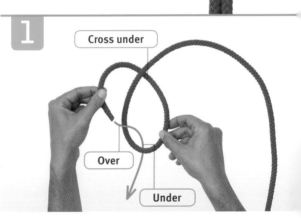

2

Over

Under

3

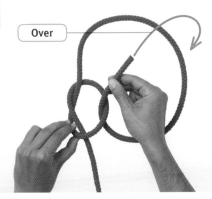

Over

4

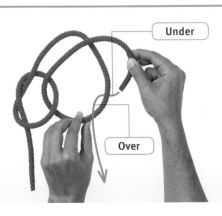

Under

Over

5

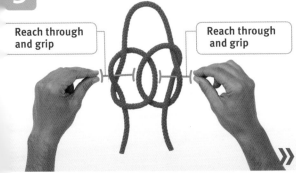

Reach through and grip

Reach through and grip

»

6

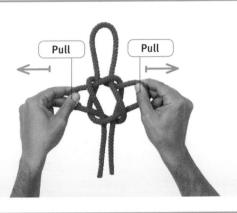

Pull   Pull

7

Pull all

8

Straighten to finish

eef Knot

- simple binding knot for securing rope around an object.
- erives its name from being tied round a bundle of sail.
- lso known as the Square Knot.

1

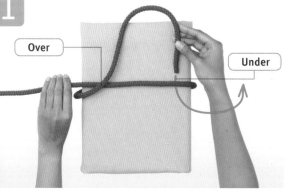

Over

Under

2

Bring together

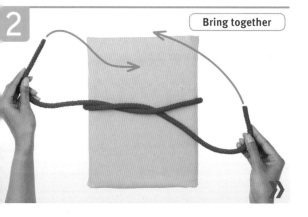

3

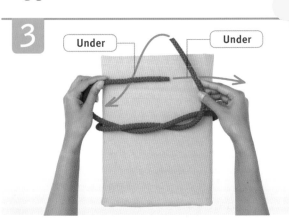

Under

Under

4

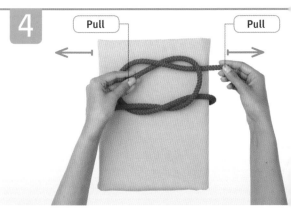

Pull

Pull

5

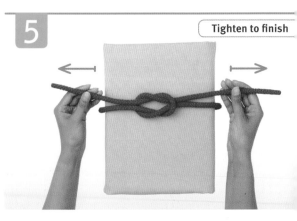

Tighten to finish

Slipped Reef Knot

A quick-release version of the Reef Knot (*see pp.85–86*).
Start with a long working end to ensure there is enough rope to form a bight.
Can be undone by tugging on the short end of the bight.

1

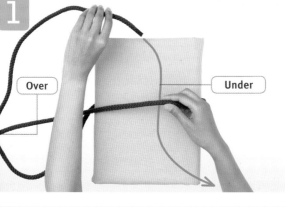

Over
Under

2

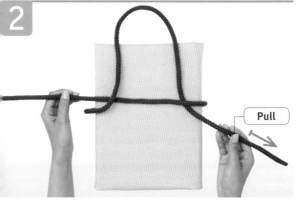

Pull

3

Form bight

4

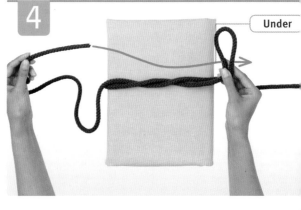

Under

5

Under

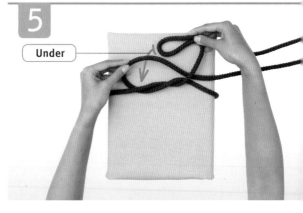

6

Over

7

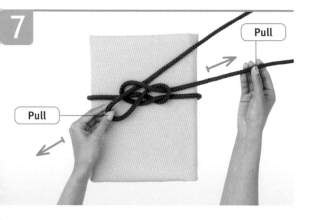

Pull

Pull

8

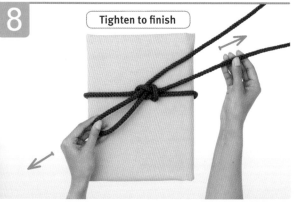

Tighten to finish

Slipped Reef Knot Doubled

- Commonly used for tying shoelaces.
- Can also be tied with ribbon to make a bow around a package.
- Formed with two bights.

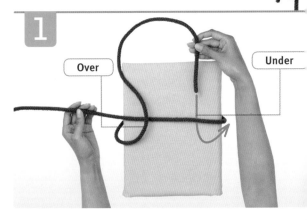

1

Over | Under

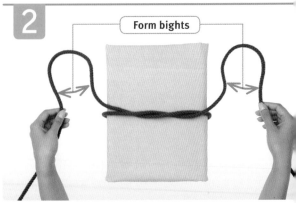

2

Form bights

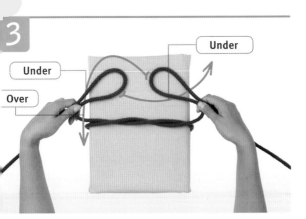

3

Under

Under

Over

4

Pull

Pull

5

Tighten to finish

Granny Knot

- An incorrectly formed version of the Reef Knot (see pp.85–86) – does not have the same square form.
- Not as stable as the Reef Knot – may slip or jam.

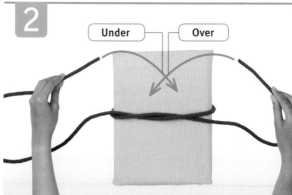

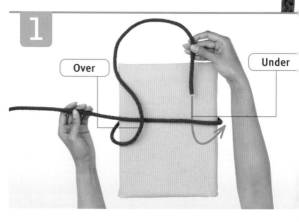

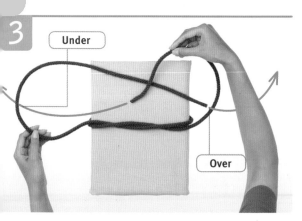

3

Under

Over

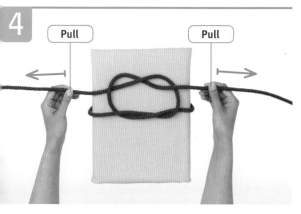

4

Pull

Pull

5

Tighten to finish

Thief Knot

- An unusual binding knot used to secure a rope or line around an object.
- Easily confused with, although much less secure than, the Reef Knot (*see pp.85–86*).
- Historically used by sailors to safeguard their bags – a thief would be likely to simply retie the bag using a Reef Knot and thus betray their presence.

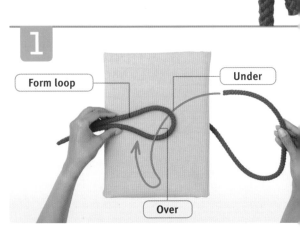

1

Form loop — Under — Over

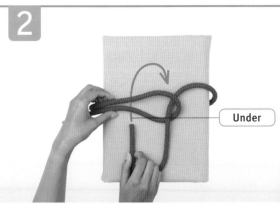

2

Under

3

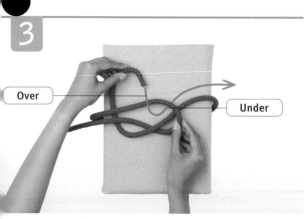

Over

Under

4

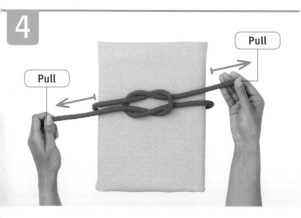

Pull

Pull

5

Tighten to finish

Surgeon's Knot

- A binding knot used by surgeons to tie sutures.
- Can also be tied around a bundle.
- If working with a bundle, draw it together by tightening the first two tucks before finishing the knot.
- The extra tuck holds the knot tight while the process is completed.

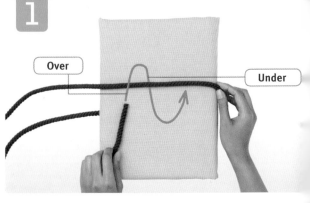

Over

Under

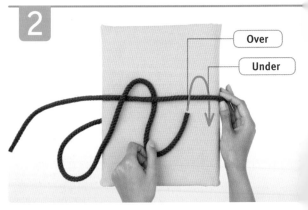

Over

Under

3

Pull

4

Bring ends together

5

Over | Under

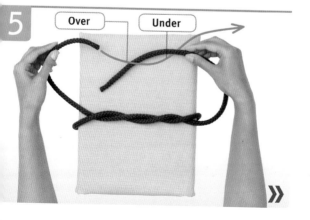

»

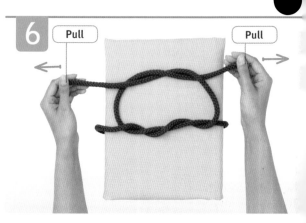

6 Pull — Pull

7 Tighten to finish

Surgeon's Knot with Second Tuck

- A surgeon's knot made with an extra tuck.
- Useful when working with slippery rope.
- Tuck the right working end twice around the left working end at Step 5 (*see p.97*).

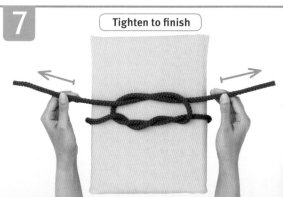

urquoise urtle

e perfect knot for tying
noelaces.

arely comes undone.

ontains elements of the Reef Knot
ee pp.85–86) and the Surgeon's
not (see pp.96–98).

undo, pull the short ends.

1

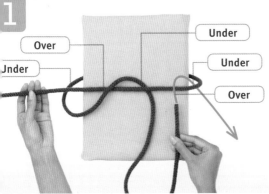

Over

Under

Under

Under

Over

2

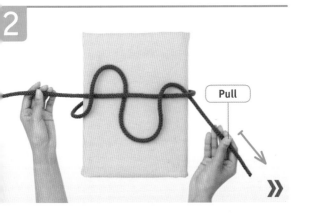

Pull

»

3

Form bight   Form bight

4

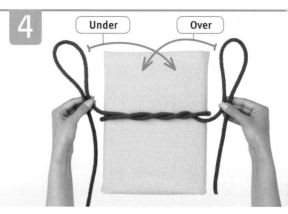

Under   Over

5

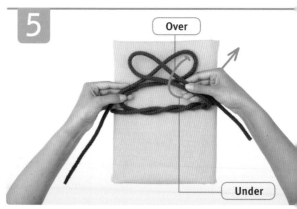

Over

Under

6

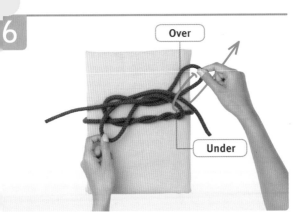

Over

Under

7

Pull

Pull

8

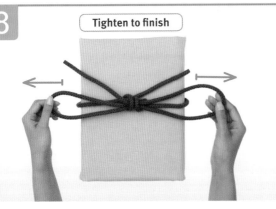

Tighten to finish

Packer's Knot

- Used to tie up a parcel or draw together a loose bundle or package.
- Based on the Figure of Eight (*see pp.38–39*).
- Secure with a half hitch (*see p.23*).

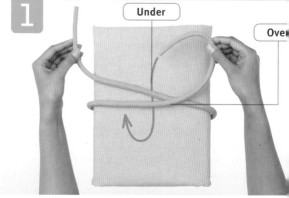

1

Under

Over

2

Over

Under

Over

3

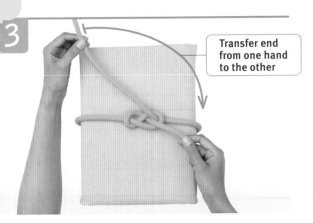

Transfer end from one hand to the other

4

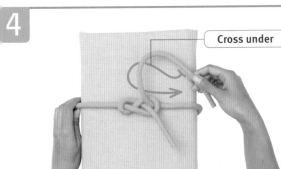

Cross under

5

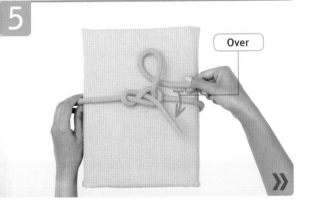

Over

»

6

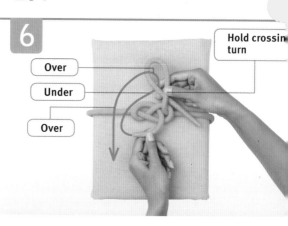

Hold crossing turn

Over

Under

Over

7

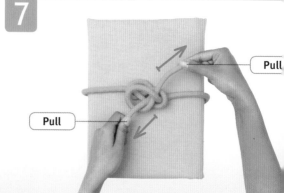

Pull

Pull

8

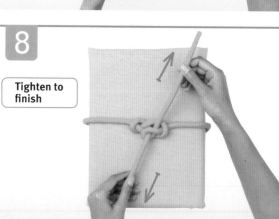

Tighten to finish

love Hitch

common, simple binding knot
sed when only one end of a rope
s available to work with.
Made from two half hitches
(see p.23), both passed
n the same direction.
Used in most lashings
(see pp.211–24).

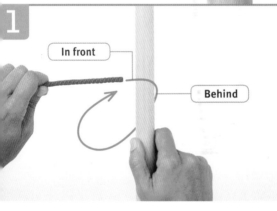

1

| In front |
| Behind |

2

| Behind |
| In front | Over |

»

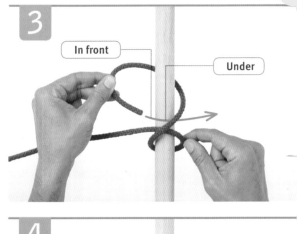

3

In front

Under

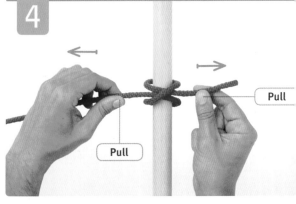

4

Pull

Pull

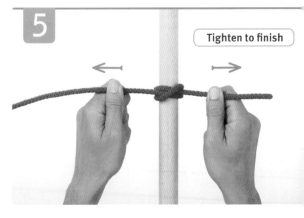

5

Tighten to finish

Clove Hitch – Second Method

A common binding knot that is quick to tie.

Can be tied in the middle of the rope.

Made from two half hitches (see p.23), both passed in the same direction.

Not completely secure – may work loose under strain.

1

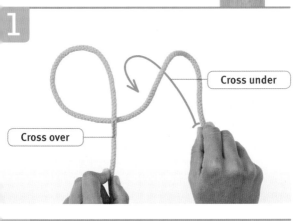

Cross over

Cross under

2

Place under — Place over

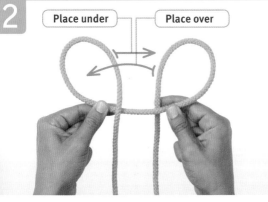

3

Arrange to form hole in centre

4

Lower onto pole

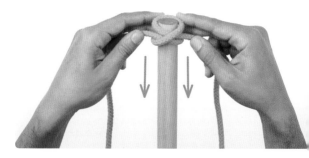

5

Tighten to finish

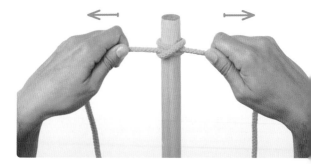

onstrictor Knot

akes a good temporary
hipping (*see p.14*)
r seizing (*see p.25*).
imple to tie but difficult
 untie.
orks best when tied in
in line.

1

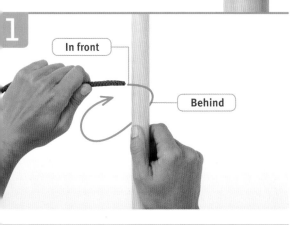

In front

Behind

2

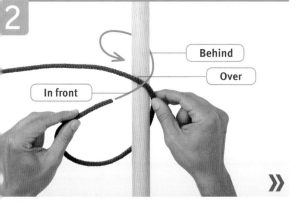

Behind

Over

In front

»

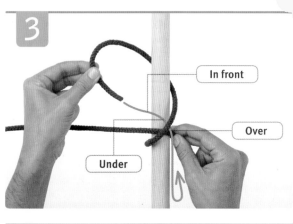

3

In front

Over

Under

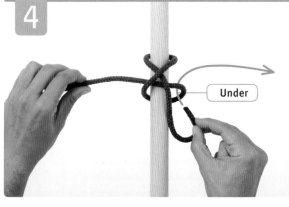

4

Under

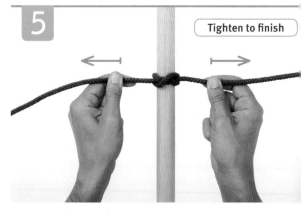

5

Tighten to finish

imber Hitch

ied around a log or a bundle
f timber.

he harder the final pull, the
ghter and more secure
he knot becomes.

he starting point for a Diagonal
ashing (*see pp.215–17*).

1

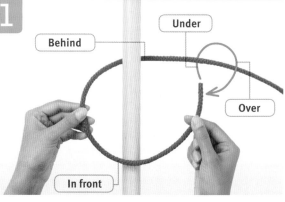

Behind

Under

Over

In front

2

Under

Over

》

3

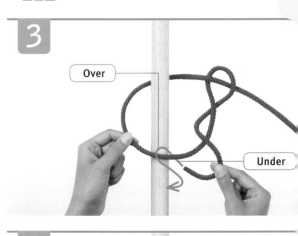

4

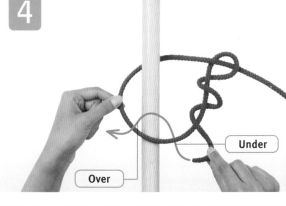

5

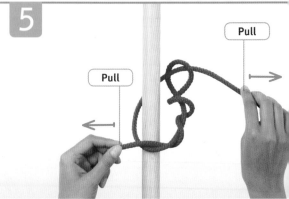

6

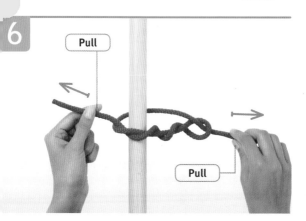

Pull

Pull

7

Tighten to finish

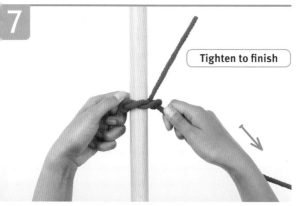

Pulling a Pole

An extra half hitch (*see p.23*) can be added to the pole if it is to be dragged through water or across land.

The half hitch prevents the pole from swaying around when it is moved.

Finish with half hitch

Boa Knot

- Used to secure or tie together cylindrical objects where a decorative as well as a practical knot is required.
- Should only be used when it can be slipped over the end of the object to which it is to be tied.
- Can be used instead of the Constrictor Knot (*see pp.109–10*).

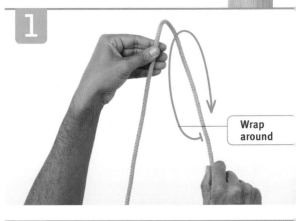

1

Wrap around

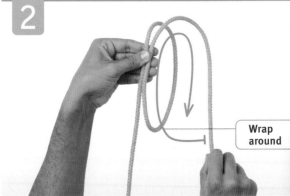

2

Wrap around

3

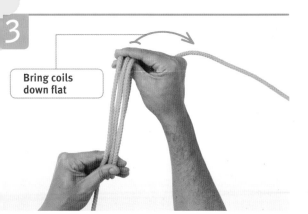

Bring coils down flat

4

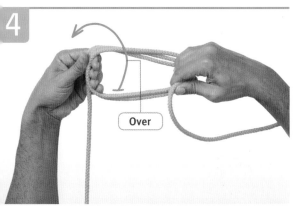

Over

5

Fold over

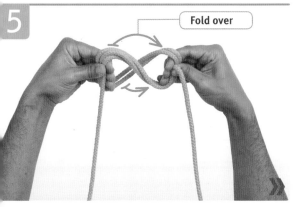

6

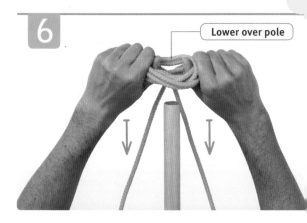

Lower over pole

7

Work into shape

8

Tighten to finish

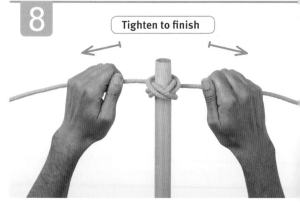

urk's Head –
hree-Lead
our-Bight

decorative knot usually tied
round a pole or rail.
an also be flattened out
to a mat.
an be doubled or tripled (*see p.24*).

(*see p.24*)

1

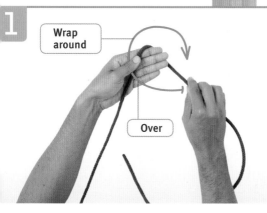

Wrap around

Over

2

Over

Under

Under

»

3

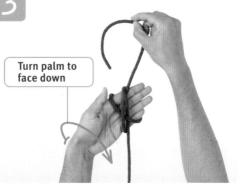

Turn palm to face down

4

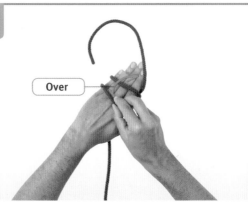

Over

5

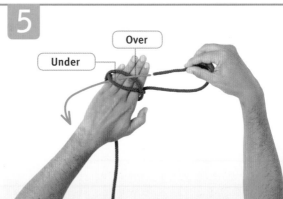

Over

Under

6

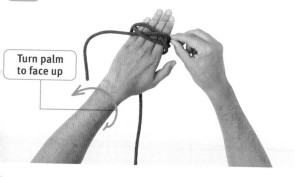

Turn palm
to face up

7

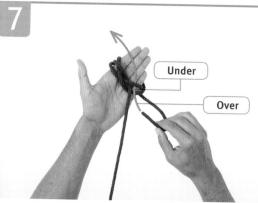

Under

Over

8

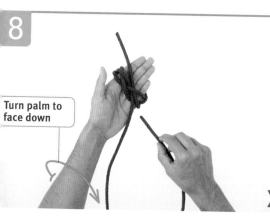

Turn palm to
face down

》

9

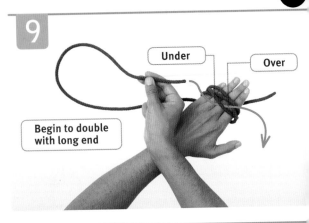

Under

Over

Begin to double with long end

10

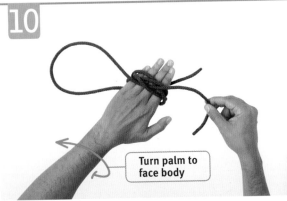

Turn palm to face body

11

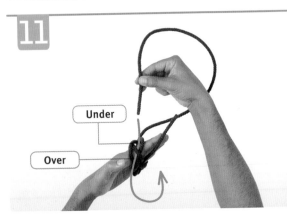

Under

Over

12

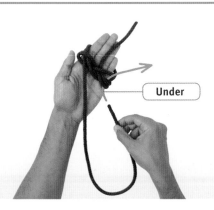

Under

13

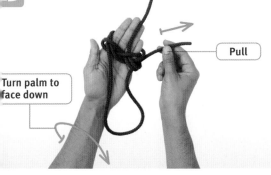

Turn palm to face down

Pull

14

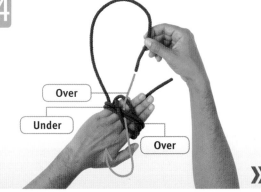

Over

Under

Over

»

15

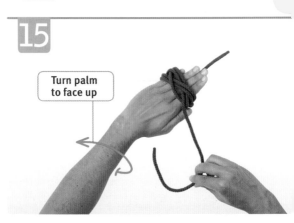

Turn palm to face up

16

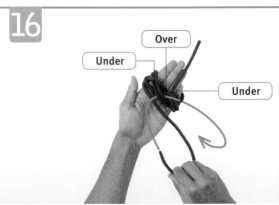

Over

Under

Under

17

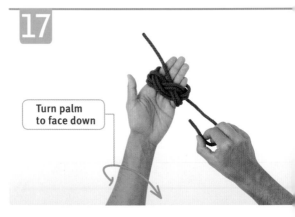

Turn palm to face down

18

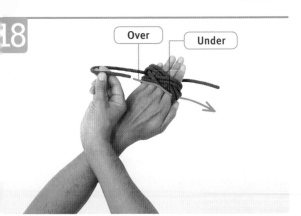

Over

Under

19

Turn palm to face up

20

Trim and tuck to finish

BEST FOR ...
Household

verday knots can be used around the home for all
inds of tasks – from hanging pictures and tying back
urtains to securing a washing line, making decorative
ows, and tying shoelaces.

ound Turn and Two
alf Hitches » pp.180–81

✓ Ideal for attaching picture
cord to the hanging rings
 screw eyes on the back of
icture frames.

✓ Also useful for tying a line
to a fixed object, such as
washing line to its pole.

✓ Can be untied even when
under strain.

Similar knots:
» pp.182–83
Buntline Hitch
» pp.184–85
Fisherman's Bend

anrope Knot » pp.61–71

✓ A perfect knot for tying
back curtains when
readed through an Eye
lice (see pp.342–46).

✓ Can also make an end
for a rope handrail.

✓ Can be made bulkier by
following the pattern
und for a third time.

Similar knots:
» pp.49–53
Monkey's Fist
» pp.72–77
Diamond Knot

Turquoise Turtle
» pp.99–101

✅ A two-loop knot that is quick to tie.

✅ Perfect for tying up the laces on shoes or boots as it rarely comes undone.

✅ Can be used to make a secure yet decorative bow on a parcel or a present.

Similar knots:
» pp.87–89
Slipped Reef Knot

Constrictor Knot
» pp.109–10

✅ A perfect replacement for a hose clip.

✅ Can also be used with stiff cord to tie up the neck of a bin bag or sack.

✅ Binds tightly, making it very hard to untie.

Similar knots:
» pp.107–08
Clove Hitch – Second Method
» pp.114–16
Boa Knot

Packer's Knot **» pp.102–04**

✅ A binding knot that is perfect for tying up a parcel, as it is easy to pull tight and lock into position.

✅ The knot's tightening feature is good for baling up bundles of newspaper.

✅ Also known as a Butcher's Knot, as it can be used to prepare joints of meat for roasting.

Similar knots:
» pp.87–89
Slipped Reef Knot
» pp.96–98
Surgeon's Knot

aggoner's Hitch
p.203–04

Pefect for tying down a load such as a pile of logs. It will undo as n as the strain is released.

Will also secure a roof box to the top of a car.

If repeatedly tied in the same place this knot can cause the e to chafe severely.

Similar knots:
》 pp.111–13
Timber hitch

Turk's Head – Four-Lead Five-Bight

- Used mainly for decorative purposes.
- Essentially a continuous Four-Strand Flat Plait (*see pp.294–95*) – can be followed around two, three, or four times.
- Adjust the spaces between the strands as you tie to ensure that they are even.

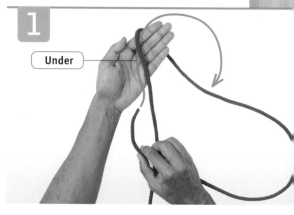

1

Under

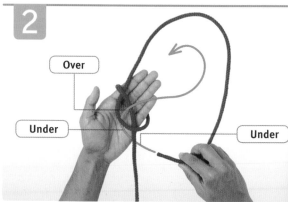

2

Over

Under

Under

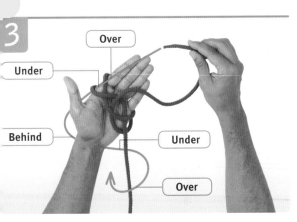

3

Over

Under

Behind

Under

Over

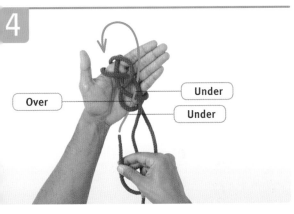

4

Over

Under

Under

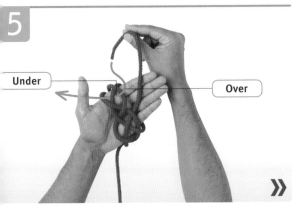

5

Under

Over

»

6

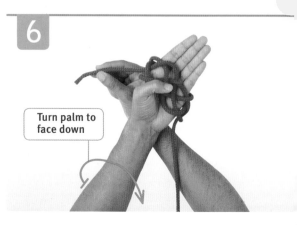

Turn palm to face down

7

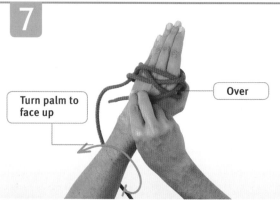

Turn palm to face up

Over

8

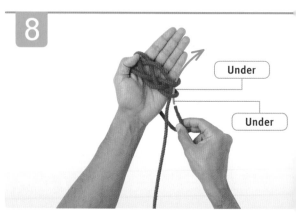

Under

Under

9

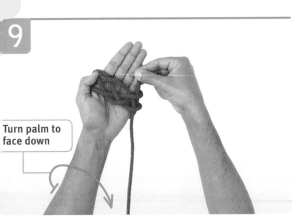

Turn palm to face down

10

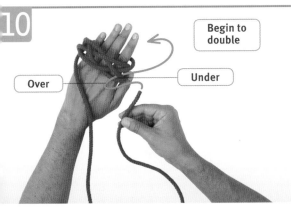

Begin to double

Over

Under

11

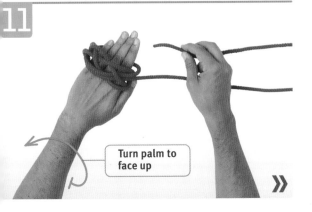

Turn palm to face up

»

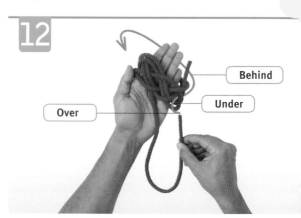

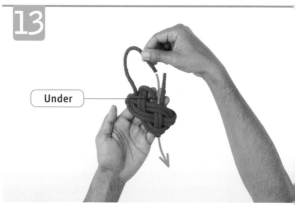

urk's Head – ive-Lead our-Bight

highly decorative knot with a large
umber of interwoven strands.
an be doubled or tripled (*see p.24*).
inish by tightening carefully then
rimming and tucking the ends inside
he knot.

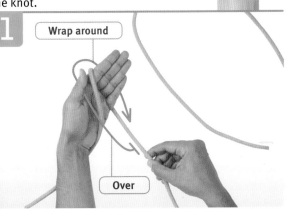

1 | Wrap around | Over

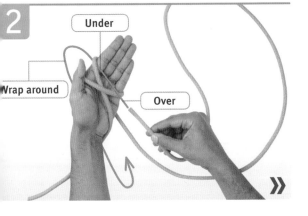

2 | Under | Wrap around | Over

»

3

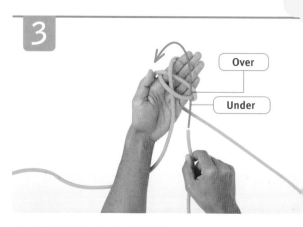

Over

Under

4

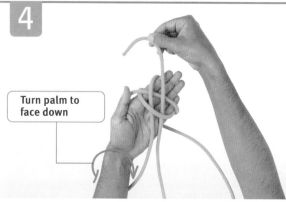

Turn palm to face down

5

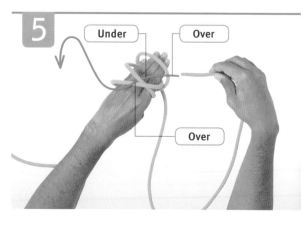

Under

Over

Over

6

Turn palm to face up

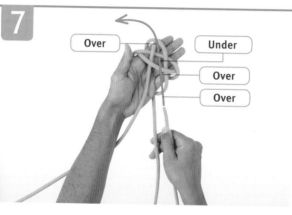

7

Over

Under

Over

Over

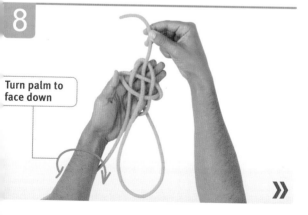

8

Turn palm to face down

»

9

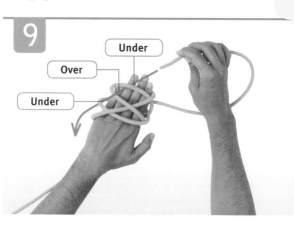

Under

Over

Under

10

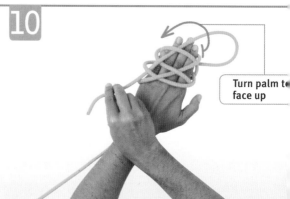

Turn palm to face up

11

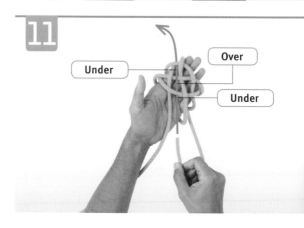

Under

Over

Under

12

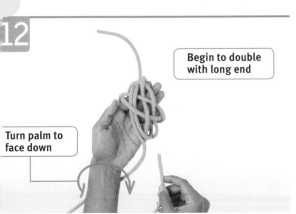

Begin to double with long end

Turn palm to face down

13

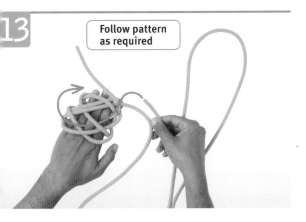

Follow pattern as required

14

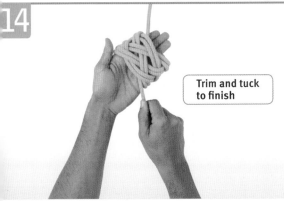

Trim and tuck to finish

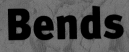

Bends

A bend is used to connect two pieces of rope or line together. Most bends are designed to tie together two ropes of equal diameter, but there are also bends that have been developed for ropes of different thicknesses.

Sheet Bend

- A common knot for joining two ropes of equal thickness.
- Quick and easy to tie.
- May work loose when not under strain.
- If joining ropes of unequal size, use the Double Sheet Bend (*see pp.144–45*).

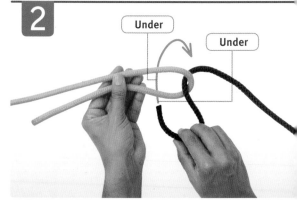

1

Form loop | Under
Over

2

Under | Under

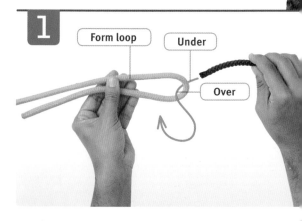

3

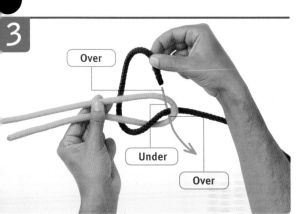

Over

Under

Over

4

Pull

5

Tighten to finish

Tucked Sheet Bend

- Used for joining two pieces of thin line.
- A variation of the Sheet Bend (*see pp.140–41*) that incorporates a Figure of Eight (*see pp.38–39*) structure.
- Tuck ends against rope to prevent snagging when pulled along.
- Will snag if pulled in the wrong direction.

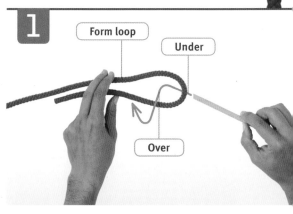

1

Form loop

Under

Over

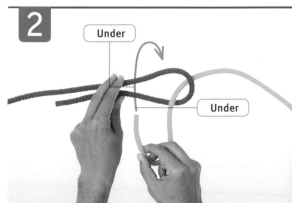

2

Under

Under

3

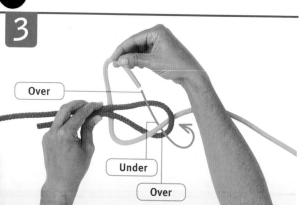

Over

Under

Over

4

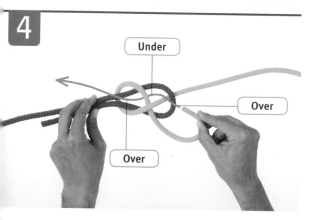

Under

Over

Over

5

Tighten to finish

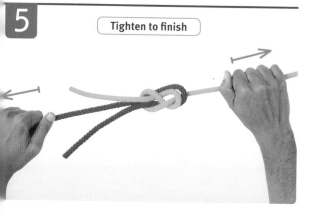

Double Sheet Bend

- Used to join two ropes of unequal thickness.
- Use the thicker rope to form the loop.

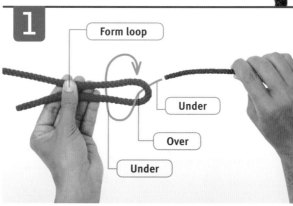

1

Form loop

Under

Over

Under

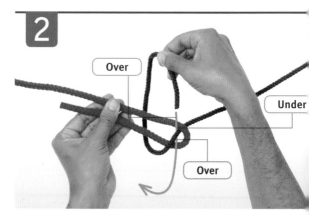

2

Over

Under

Over

3

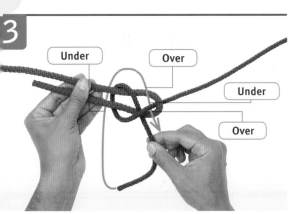

Under

Over

Under

Over

4

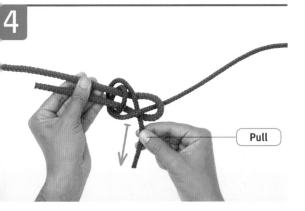

Pull

5

Tighten to finish

Rope Yarn Knot

- Used for tying together rope yarns to make a new piece of rope.
- Can also be used to join textile materials together.
- Similar in structure to the Reef Knot (*see pp.85–86*) but less bulky.

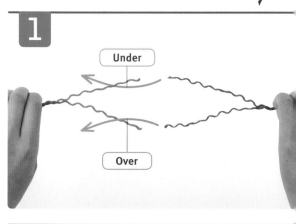

1

Under

Over

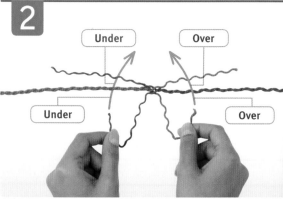

2

Under

Over

Under

Over

3

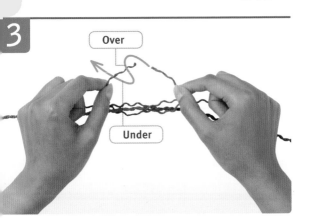

Over

Under

4

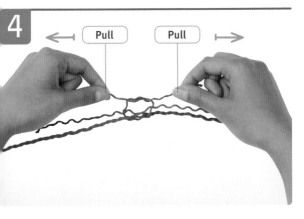

Pull

Pull

5

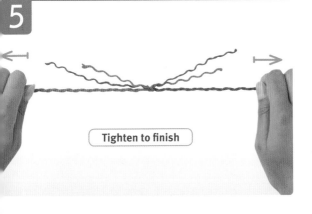

Tighten to finish

Carrick Bend

- Good for joining two thick ropes or cables.
- Can be seized (*see p.25*) as a flat knot, or tightened to collapse on itself.
- Easy to untie.

1

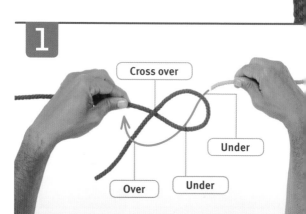

Cross over

Under

Under

Over

Under

2

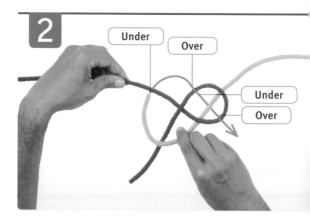

Under

Over

Under

Over

3

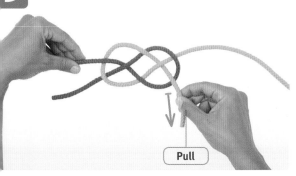

Pull

4

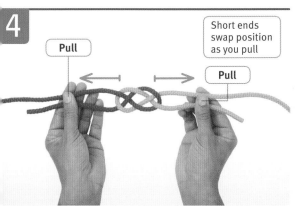

Pull

Short ends swap position as you pull

Pull

5

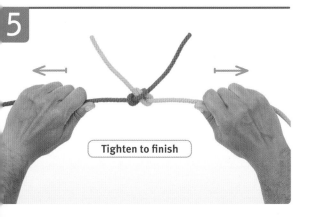

Tighten to finish

Hunter's Bend

- Good for joining two lengths of synthetic rope (*see also pp.140–41*).
- Needs to be carefully adjusted to shape.
- Also known as the Rigger's Bend.
- Named after Dr Edward Hunter.

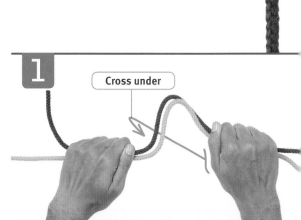

1 Cross under

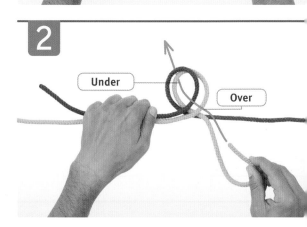

2 Under · Over

3

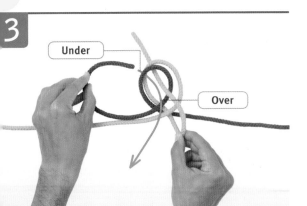

Under

Over

4

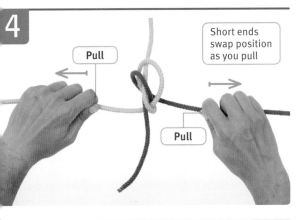

Pull

Short ends swap position as you pull

Pull

5

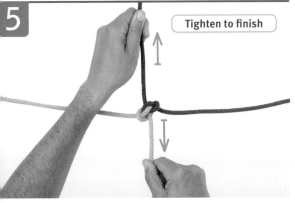

Tighten to finish

Lanyard Knot

- A decorative method for joining two ropes.
- Based on the same structure as the Carrick Bend (*see pp.148–49*).
- Also known as the Friendship Knot.

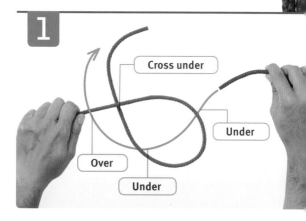

1

Cross under

Under

Over

Under

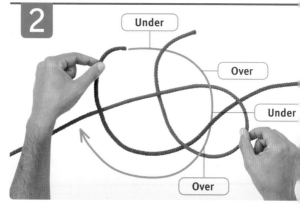

2

Under

Over

Under

Over

3

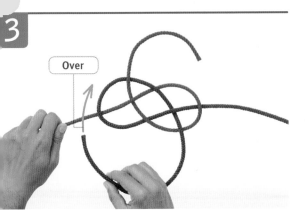

Over

4

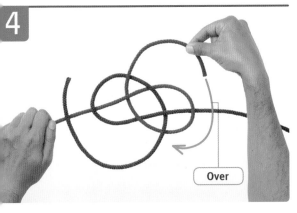

Over

5

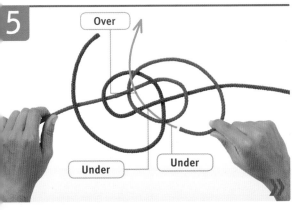

Over

Under

Under

6

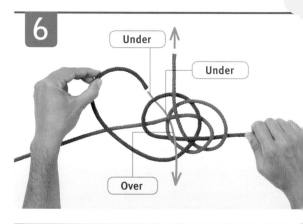

Under

Under

Over

7

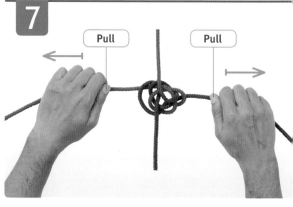

Pull

Pull

8

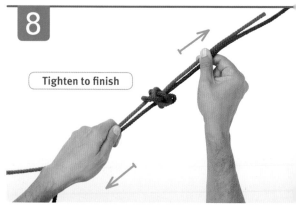

Tighten to finish

shley's Bend

Jsed to join two pieces of
hin line together.

:asy to tie and untie.

Secure even when subjected
o strenuous movement.

:nsure that both crossing turns
ire the same.

Jamed after Clifford W. Ashley,
in American knot expert.

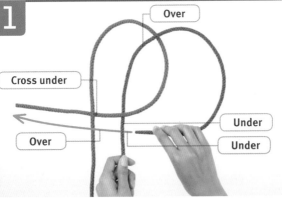

1

Over

Cross under

Over

Under

Under

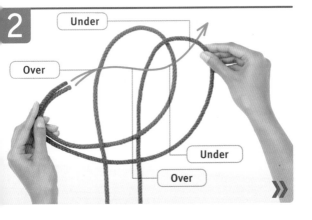

2

Under

Over

Under

Over

3

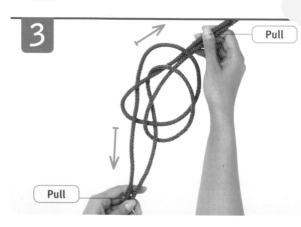

Pull

Pull

4

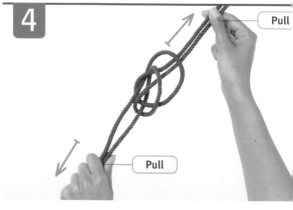

Pull

Pull

5

Tighten to finish

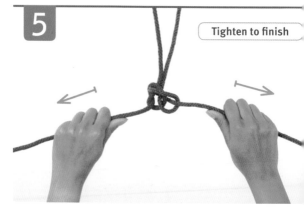

Fisherman's Knot

Good for joining relatively thin ropes and lines.

Used by fishermen and climbers.

Ensure that the lengths of the short ends are at least five times the diameter of the rope.

Consists of two sliding Overhand Knots (*see pp.28–29*).

1

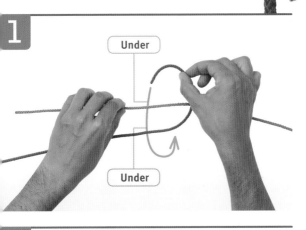

Under

Under

2

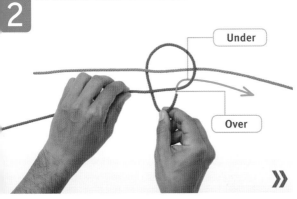

Under

Over

»

3

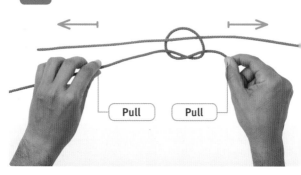

Pull | Pull

4

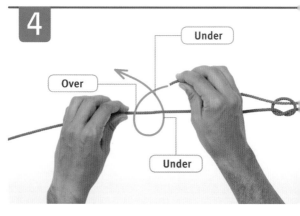

Under

Over

Under

5

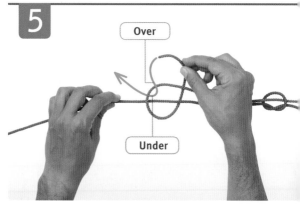

Over

Under

6

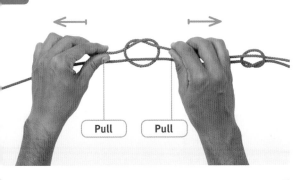

Pull   Pull

7

Bring knots together

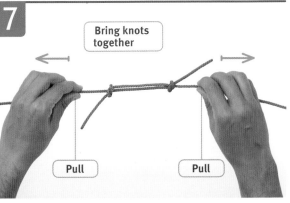

Pull   Pull

8

Tighten to finish

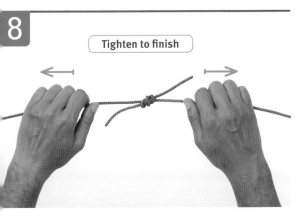

Double Fisherman's Knot

- Used when a rope or line is particularly slippery.
- The extra turns prevent the knot from coming undone when put under strain.
- The ends may be taped down for greater security.

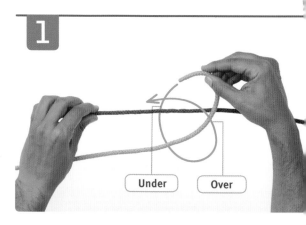

Under | Over

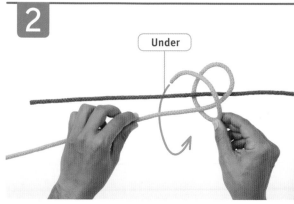

Under

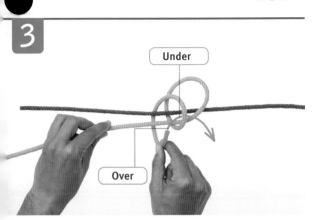

3

Under

Over

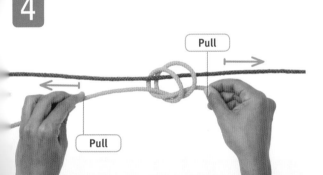

4

Pull

Pull

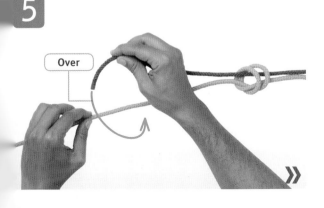

5

Over

》

6

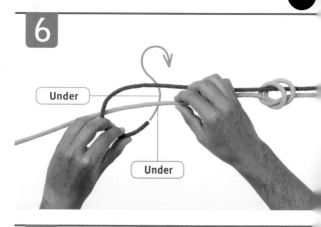

Under

Under

7

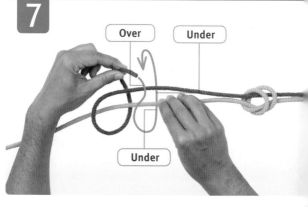

Over   Under

Under

8

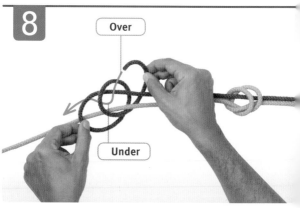

Over

Under

9

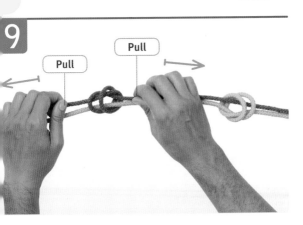

Pull Pull

10

Bring knots together

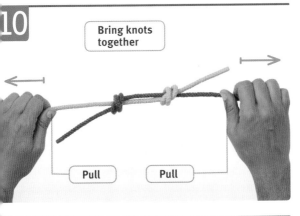

Pull Pull

11

Tighten to finish

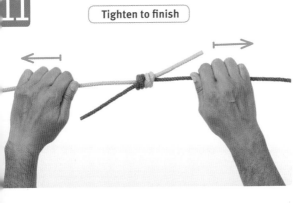

EST FOR ...
limbing

nowledge of knots is essential for climbers, as their
ety may depend on it. It is important to take care when
shing these common climbing knots – check the shape
orrect and make sure there are no twists in the rope.

lian Hitch
p.234–35

Used on a safety line
by climbers as it can
trol the speed of a fall
the distance fallen.

A knot that can also be
used for abseiling.

Creates twists in the rope and
causes wear, so best used as
ckup or in an emergency.

Similar knots:
**» p.235 Reversed
Italian Hitch**

usik Knot » pp.228–29

Will slide when not under strain,
so useful for providing handholds
footholds on ascent and descent.

Extra turns can be added to
give more friction if the
e is slippery or wet.

Always
check
t the knot
ecure and
ds under strain.

Similar knots:
**» pp.232–33
Klemheist Knot**

Figure-of-Eight Loop
» pp.249–50

✓ Popular among climbers as its distinctive shape makes it easy to check that it has been tied properly.

✓ Still possesses some residual strength as an overhand loop, even if it is not tied properly.

Similar kn•
» pp.240–4
Bowline
» pp.253–5
Overhand L•

Double Fisherman's Knot » pp.160–63

✓ Excellent for making continuous loops for Prusik slings (see pp.228–29).

✓ Also good for joining two lengths of rope, even if they are of different diameters.

✓ The chance of snagging can be reduced by taping the ends.

Similar knots
» pp.157–59
Fisherman's Kn•
» pp.172–73
Water Knot

pine Butterfly » pp.238–39

Can be quickly tied in the middle of the rope without needing to e access to either of the rope ends.

Ideal for attaching a middleman on a climb as strain can be lied to er side he knot.

Similar knots:
>> pp.249–50
Figure-of-
Eight Loop
>> pp.259–61
Bowline on
the Bight

wline with Stopper
.248

A variation on a Bowline which kes a good stopper he end of a rope.

Bulky and, when tight, easier to ie than a Figure ight or a Double rhand Knot.

Similar knots:
>> pp.242–44
Bowline –
Second
Method
>> pp.245–
47 Bowline
with Two
Turns

Blood Knot

- An effective method for joining together two pieces of thin line, such as fishing line.
- If tying with nylon, moisten the line to help draw it tight.
- Almost impossible to untie.
- Also known as the Barrel Knot.

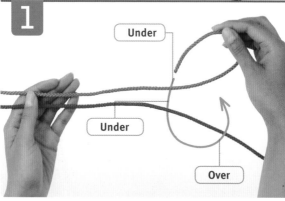

1

Under

Under

Over

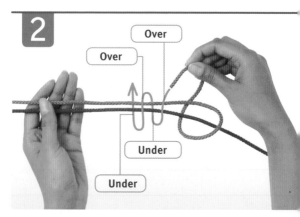

2

Over

Over

Under

Under

3

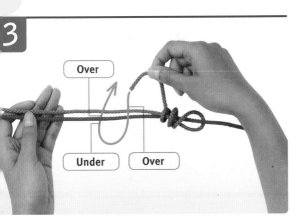

Over

Under Over

4

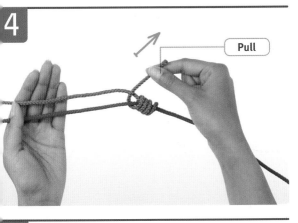

Pull

5

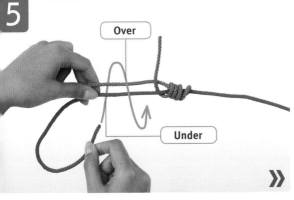

Over

Under

»

6

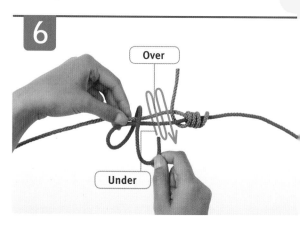

Over

Under

7

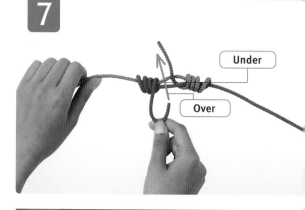

Under

Over

8

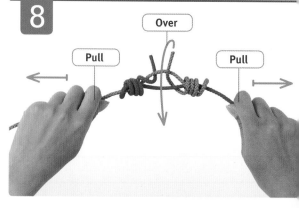

Over

Pull

Pull

9

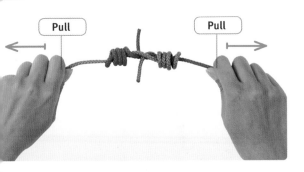

Pull | Pull

10

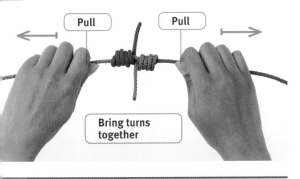

Pull | Pull

Bring turns together

11

Trim short ends to finish, if required

Water Knot

- Good for binding two ropes together.
- Will also work well with climber's flat tape.
- Work into a neat, flat arrangement.
- Based on the structure of the Overhand Knot (*see pp.28–29*).
- Also known as the Double Overhand Bend.

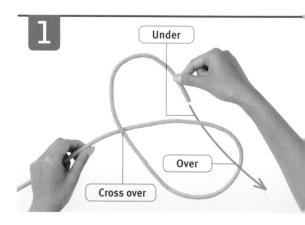

1

Under

Over

Cross over

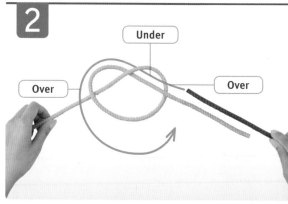

2

Under

Over

Over

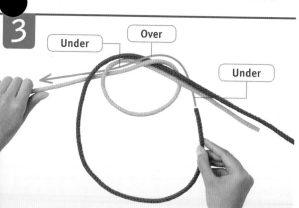

3

Under | Over | Under

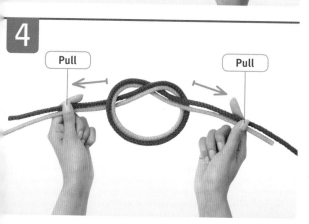

4

Pull | Pull

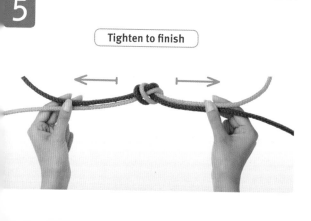

5

Tighten to finish

Hitches

A hitch is tied to secure a rope to an object, such as a pole or ring. Many hitches – especially those that are used by sailors – are designed to be both quick to tie and easy to undo.

Rolling Hitch

- Can be used to take strain off another rope or pole.
- Suitable for use when the pull on the rope is coming from a low angle, or from the side.
- Will only slide in one direction along the pole or rope.
- Will lock if pulled in the other direction.

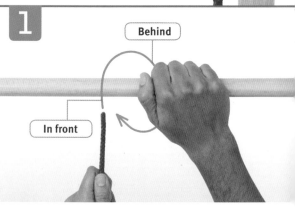

1

Behind

In front

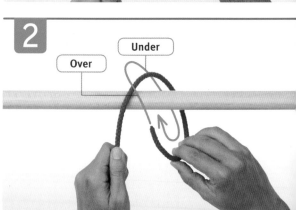

2

Over

Under

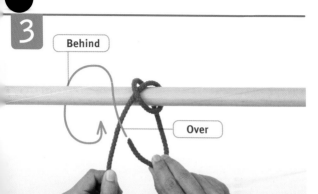

3

Behind

Over

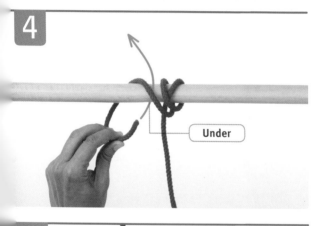

4

Under

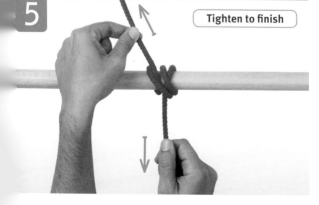

5

Tighten to finish

Mirrored Rolling Hitch

- Used to tie a rope to a pole or to take strain off another rope.
- Ensure that the second turn locks over the first.
- Make sure that the knot is tight before applying strain.
- Not suitable for stiff or slippery ropes.

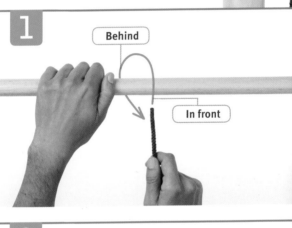

1

Behind

In front

2

Behind

Over

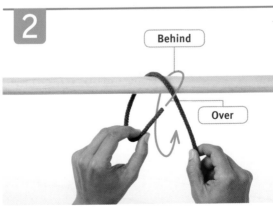

3

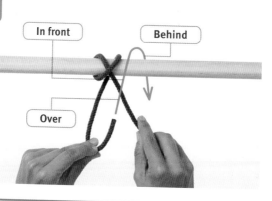

In front

Behind

Over

4

Under

5

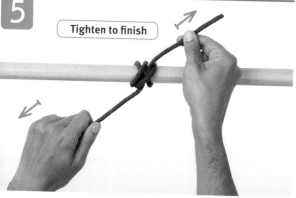

Tighten to finish

Round Turn and Two Half Hitches

- Used to secure a rope to a fixed object, such as a pole or ring.
- Easy to tie.
- Ensure that you make the half hitches (*see p.23*) in the same direction.

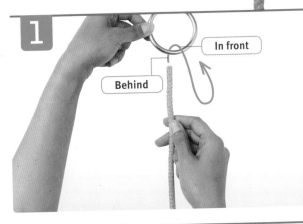

1

In front

Behind

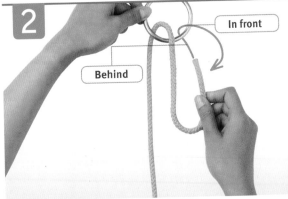

2

In front

Behind

3

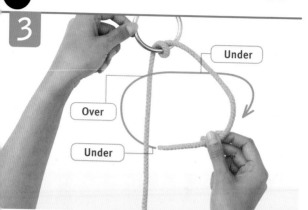

Under

Over

Under

4

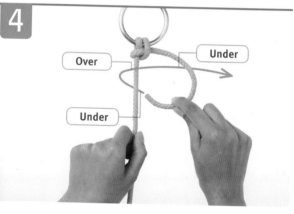

Over

Under

Under

5

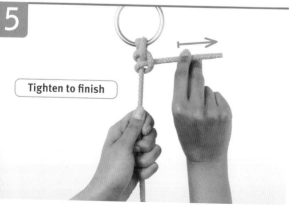

Tighten to finish

Buntline Hitch

- Used to attach a rope to an object such as a ring or pole.
- Will not come undone even when subjected to a lot of movement.
- Works well with hi-tech rope, such as Kevlar.

1

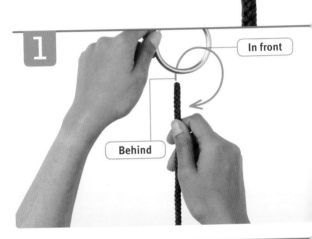

In front

Behind

2

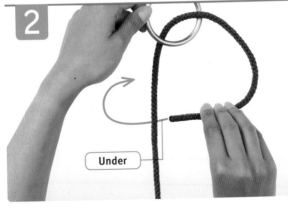

Under

3

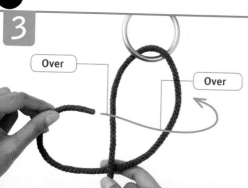

Over

Over

4

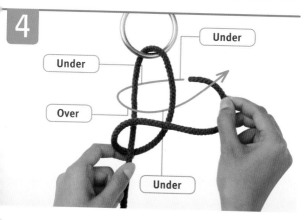

Under

Under

Over

Under

5

Tighten to finish

Fisherman's Bend

- Good for tying a rope to an anchor or a buoy.
- Easy to untie.
- Seize (*see pp.387–89*) the working end to the standing part to make more secure.
- Also known as the Anchor Bend.

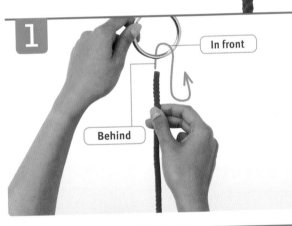

1

In front

Behind

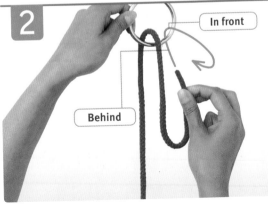

2

In front

Behind

3

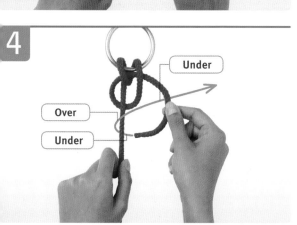

Over

Under

Over

Under

Under

4

Under

Over

Under

5

Tighten to finish

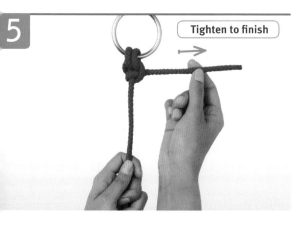

EST FOR ...
amping

ew simple knots can make camping much easier
d safer. They can be helpful in pitching a tent and
nsporting equipment and, in survival situations, can
used to make a shelter or lash a tarpaulin to trees.

olling Hitch » pp.176–77

A hitch that can be used
to secure guy ropes to a
t peg.

Can be used to apply
tension to a line if your
y ropes do not have an
juster.

Strain can be applied
horizontally in one
ection, or vertically.

Similar knots:
» pp.178–79
Mirrored
Rolling Hitch

heer Lashing
pp.222–24

A lashing that is perfect
for making the frame
a shelter.

Can also be used to
attach a reinforcing piece
wood to a broken pole.

If tied loosely at the end
of two poles, it can be
ened out into an A-frame.

Similar knots:
» pp.211–14
Square Lashing

Square Lashing
» pp.211–14

✓ A good multi-purpose, load-bearing lashing used to tie two poles together at right angles.

✓ Can be used to build rigid structures of all sizes – useful for a temporary table or stand while camping.

Similar knots:
» pp.215–17
Diagonal Lashin[g]

Round Turn and Two Half Hitches » pp.180–81

✓ The perfect knot for attaching a line to a ring, pole, or post.

✓ Can support heavy loads, so is ideal for fastening a rope swing to a branch of a tree.

✓ Can also be used to secure a guy rope to a tent peg.

Similar knots:
» pp.184–85
Fisherman's Bend

Bowline » pp.240–41

✓ A simple knot for tying a loop around a fixed object.

✓ Good for tying tarpaulins or sheets – it won't slip or jam easily in windy conditions.

✓ Can also be used to hang a hammock, or attach a canoe to a trailer.

Similar knots
» pp.245–47
Bowline with
Two Turns
» pp.249–5[ ]
Figure-of-Ei[ght]
Loop

Waggoner's Hitch

》 pp.203–04

✓ Used for centuries to fasten loads onto wagons and trucks, t will secure a load tightly to a roof ack or trailer.

✓ Use where a rope needs to be pulled extra tight – the knot's ever-type action allows strain to e put on a rope.

Similar knots:
》 pp.211–14
Square Lashing
》 pp.222–24
Sheer Lashing

Cow Hitch

- Used to tie a rope around a ring or pole.
- Formed with two half hitches (*see p.23*) tied in opposite directions.
- The least secure of all hitches unless used with a fixed loop.
- Also known as the Lark's Head.

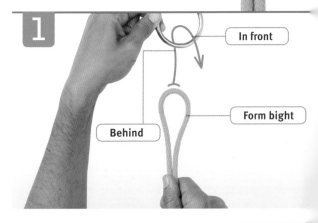

1

In front

Behind

Form bight

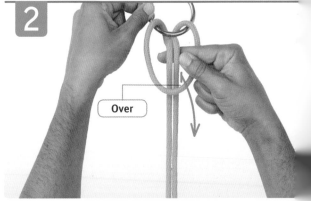

2

Over

3

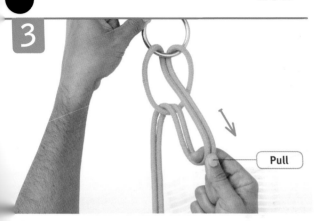

Pull

4

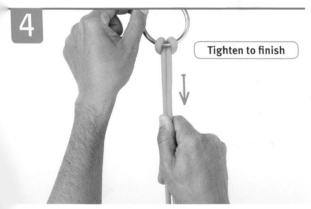

Tighten to finish

Pedigree Cow Hitch

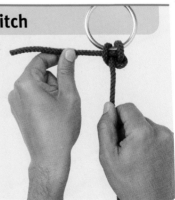

- If only one standing part of a Cow Hitch (*see pp.190–91*) is taking strain, make it more secure by tucking the other part between the bight and ring.

- Ensure the tail is long, so it does not pull out if strain is applied.

Cow Hitch with Toggle

- Variation of a Cow Hitch (*see pp.190–91*) used when there is no access to the working end of the rope.
- Remove the toggle for quick release.

1

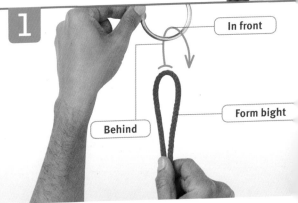

In front

Form bight

Behind

2

Straighten

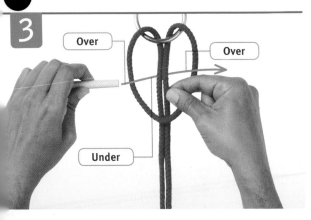

3

Over

Over

Under

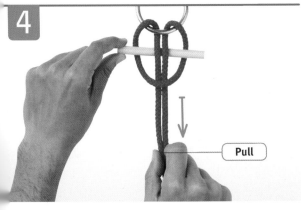

4

Pull

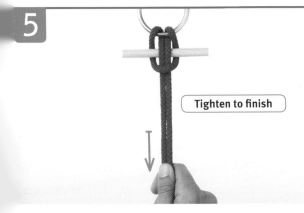

5

Tighten to finish

Sheepshank

- Used to shorten a rope without cutting it and to relieve the strain on worn-out parts of a rope.
- Ensure that the rope is taut to avoid slackening of the knot.
- Seize (*see pp.387–89*) the end loops to the standing parts of the rope for greater security.

1

Cross under

Cross under twice

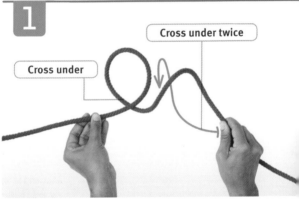

2

Reach through and grip

3

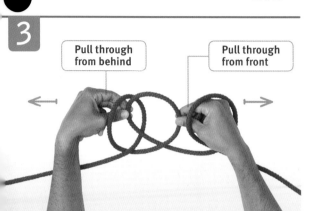

Pull through from behind

Pull through from front

4

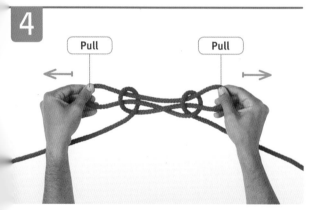

Pull

Pull

5

Tighten to finish

Sheepshank Man o' War

- Used to shorten a rope or to relieve tension on a worn-out part of rope.
- A secure version of the Sheepshank (*see pp.194–95*) that is easy to untie.
- Made with four half hitches (*see p.23*).
- Seize (*see pp.387–89*) the end loops to the standing parts for greater security.

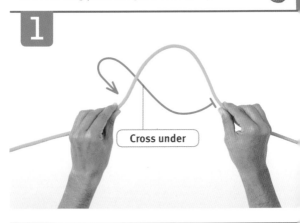

1

Cross under

2

Cross under three times

3

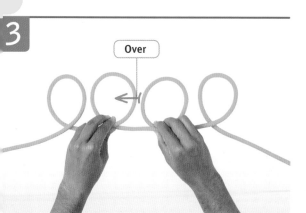

Over

4

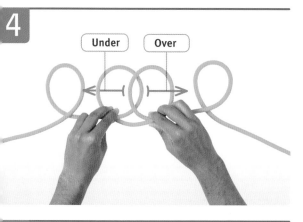

Under   Over

5

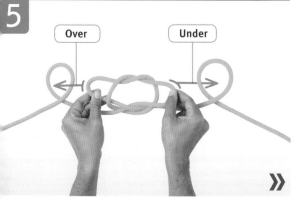

Over   Under

»

6

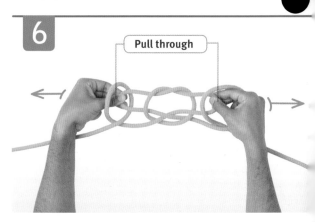

Pull through

7

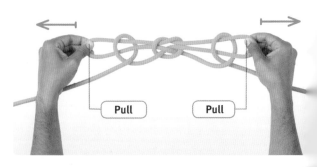

Pull   Pull

8

Tighten to finish

Marlinespike Hitch

Useful for pulling on a thin line or rope.

Quick and easy to tie – the knot disappears when the spike is removed.

Can only be pulled in one direction.

A marlinespike (*see p.19*) is not essential – will work with any type of rod or spike.

1

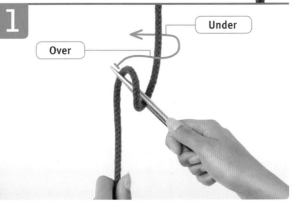

Under

Over

2

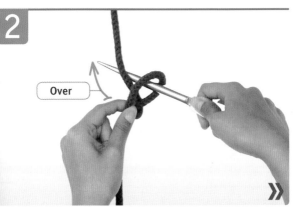

Over

»

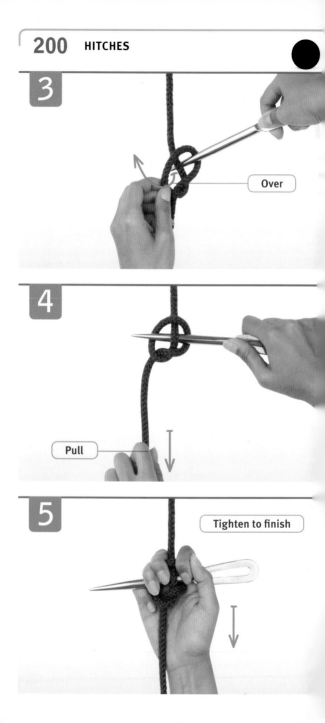

3

Over

4

Pull

5

Tighten to finish

Highwayman's Hitch

quick-release hitch.
used to tether horses.
nsure that the strain is placed
n the standing part.
ull the short end to release.

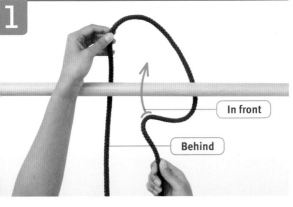

1

In front

Behind

2

Over

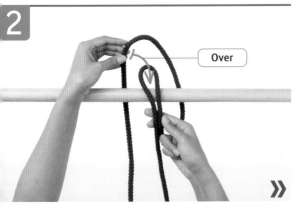

»

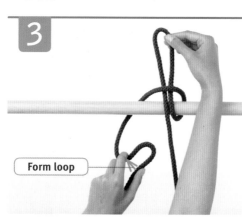

3

Form loop

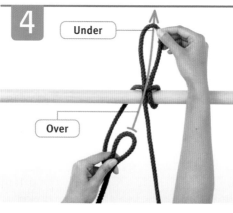

4

Under

Over

5

Tighten to finish

Waggoner's Hitch

Allows strain to be put on a length of rope.
Traditionally used to secure loads on
wagons and lorries.

Will come undone as soon as the tension
is removed.

Constant use of this hitch in the same place
on the rope can lead to rapid wear.

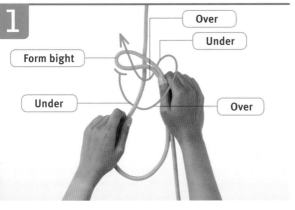

1

Over

Under

Form bight

Under

Over

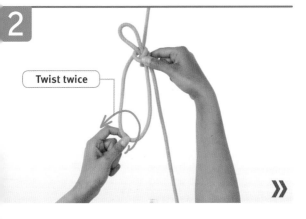

2

Twist twice

»

3

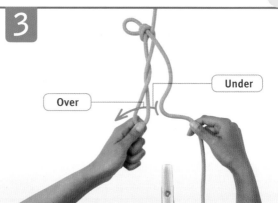

Over

Under

4

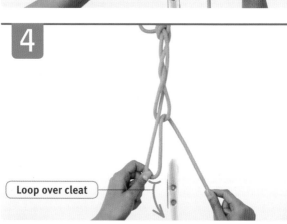

Loop over cleat

5

Tighten to finish

Snelling a Hook

Used to bind a fishing line to a hook.
Can also be used to attach a line to
a hook without an eye, known as a
spade-ended hook.

Moisten the nylon line to help
draw it tight.

1

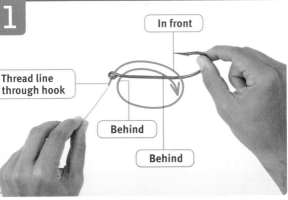

Thread line
through hook

In front

Behind

Behind

2

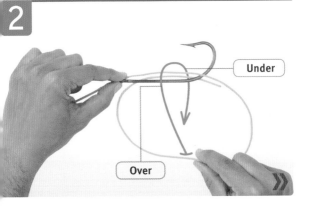

Under

Over

3

Wrap around several times

Under

Over

4

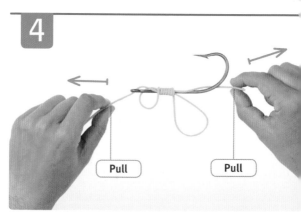

Pull

Pull

5

Tighten to finish

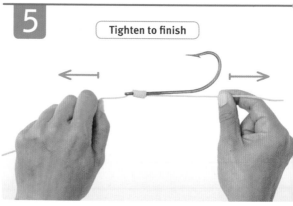

'linch Knot

Jsed to tie fishing line
o the eye of a hook.
'or thicker lines, wrap around
our times only.
Moisten the line before working
he knot into shape.

1

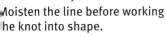

Thread line through hook

2

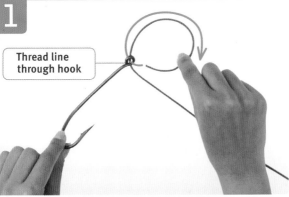

Wrap around at least six times

Over

Under

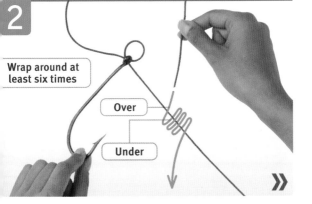

»

3

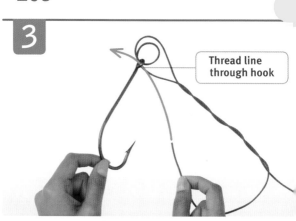

Thread line through hook

4

Tighten and trim to finish

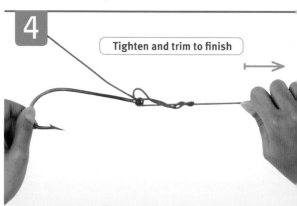

Improved Clinch Knot

- Used for particularly thin and slippery fishing line.

- The extra tuck gives additional security and prevents the knot from coming undone.

Over

Under

Palomar Knot

Used to secure a fishing
line to a hook or lure.
A strong knot that works
with slippery nylon line.
Difficult to untie.
Moisten the line to help
draw it tight.

1

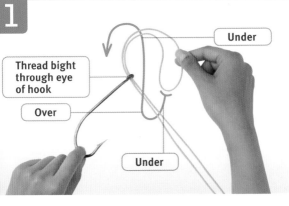

Under

**Thread bight
through eye
of hook**

Over

Under

2

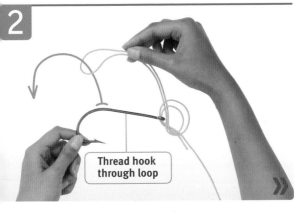

**Thread hook
through loop**

3

Pull

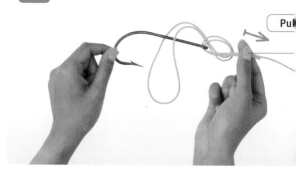

4

Pull

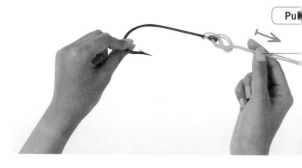

5

Tighten to finish

Square Lashing

Used to lash together two poles crossing at right angles.

Pull tight each turn before proceeding to the next one.

Start and finish with a Clove Hitch (*see pp.105–06*).

Ensure that the first Clove Hitch is tied below the horizontal pole.

Tighten by making two turns across the lashing (frapping turns).

1 TIE A CLOVE HITCH (》pp.105–06)

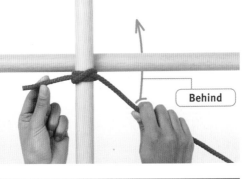

Behind

2

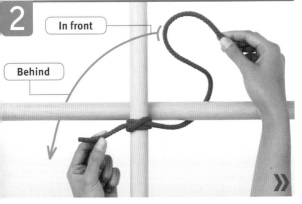

In front

Behind

》

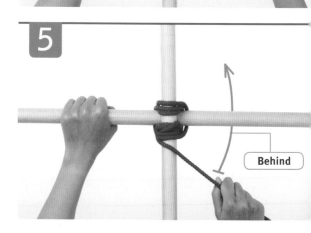

3

In front

4

In front
Behind
Wrap around twice
Behind
In front

5

Behind

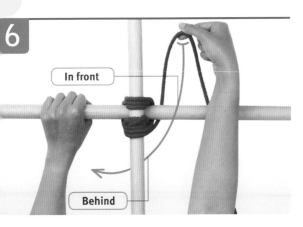

6

In front

Behind

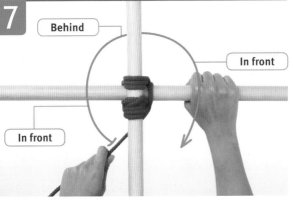

7

Behind

In front

In front

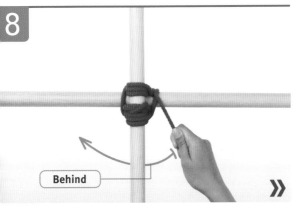

8

Behind

»

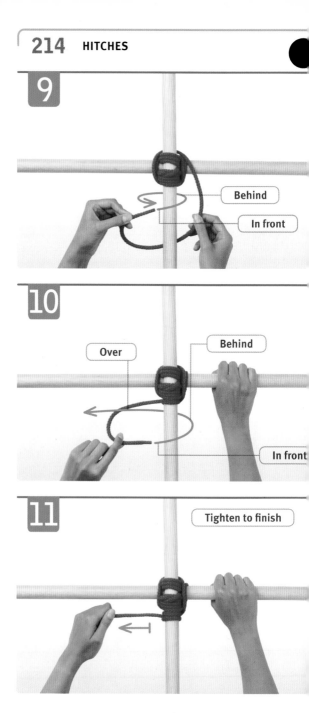

9

Behind

In front

10

Over

Behind

In front

11

Tighten to finish

iagonal ashing

sed to lash together two
iagonal poles.

efore you start, ensure there
; enough rope to complete
ie lashing.

ghten with two turns across
ie lashing (frapping turns).

nish with a Clove Hitch
ee pp.105–06).

1 TIE A TIMBER HITCH (»pp.111–13)

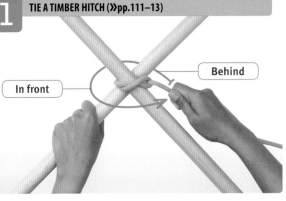

In front

Behind

2

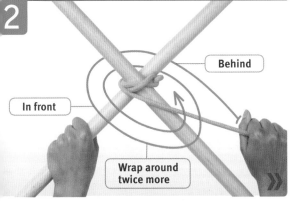

In front

Behind

Wrap around
twice more

»

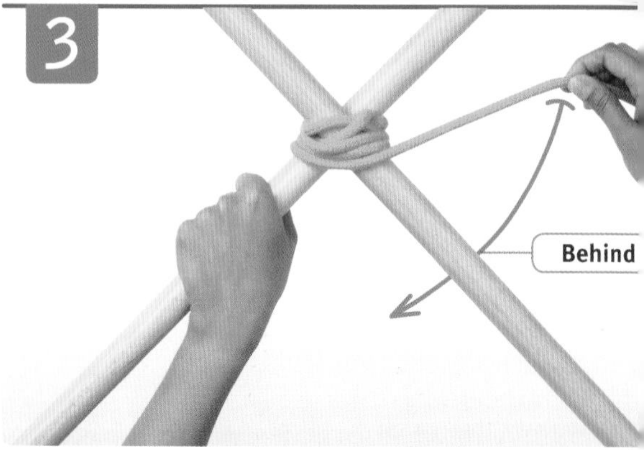

3

Behind

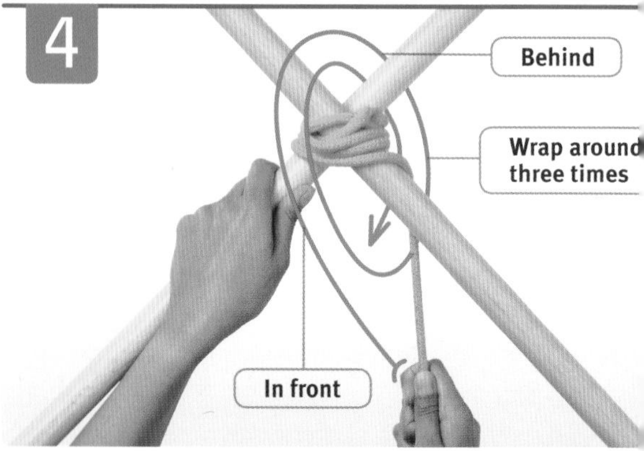

4

Behind

Wrap around three times

In front

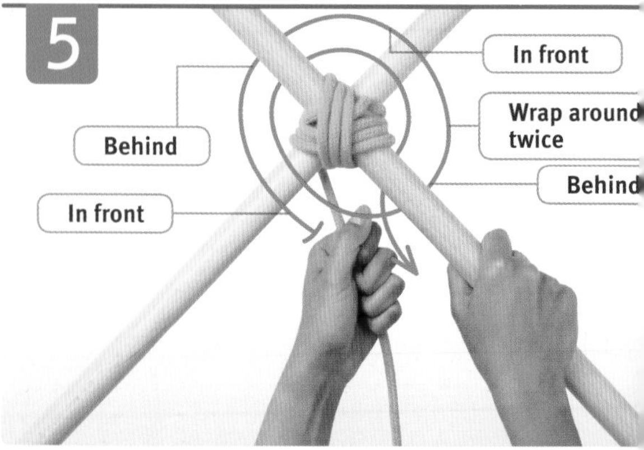

5

In front

Wrap around twice

Behind

Behind

In front

6

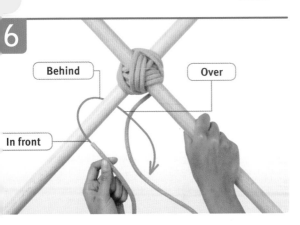

Behind

Over

In front

7

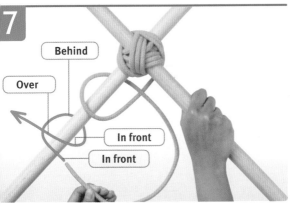

Behind

Over

In front

In front

8

Tighten to finish

EST FOR ...
Gardening

ere are several uses for knots around the garden,
m simple jobs like tying a plant to a support, to
ger tasks such as lashing canes together to make
ellis or fixing a swing to a tree.

nstrictor Knot
p.109–10

Good for fixing a hose
in position if you do not
e a hose clip.

Can also be used to
draw together a bundle
objects such as logs.

Difficult to untie once it
has been put under strain –
ay need to be cut.

Similar knots:
**》 pp.105–06
Clove Hitch
》 pp.114–16
Boa Knot**

heer Lashing
p.222–23

The perfect knot for
tying two canes together
make a support for a plant.

Can also be used with
thinner line to tie a
pling to a support post.

Similar
knots:
**》 pp.211–14
Square
Lashing
》 pp.215–17
Diagonal
Lashing**

Round Turn and Two Half Hitches » pp.180–81

✓ Useful for tying a line to a ring or post.

✓ Can also be used to tie a swing to a tree branch.

✗ If used for a swing, padding may need to be placed under the rope to protect the tree.

Similar knots:
» pp.182–83
Buntline Hitch
» pp.184–85
Fisherman's Bend

Square Lashing
» pp.211–14

✓ Good for making support frames for vegetables such as beans or tomatoes.

✓ Can also be used to make a trellis.

✓ Add frapping turns to make the knot more secure.

Similar knots
» pp.215–17
Diagonal Lashing
» pp.222–23
Sheer Lashing

Timber Hitch
» p.111–13

✓ A good hitch for tying up bundles of branches, as its tightening action increases with strain.

✓ Can be finished with a half hitch for extra security when dragging larger loads, or transporting a bundle over a long distance.

Similar knots:
» pp.109–10
Constrictor Knot

Sheet Bend
» pp.140–41

✓ Best used for joining ropes together because is quick and easy to tie, and unlikely to untie accidentally.

✗ A Double Sheet Bend is required when joining ropes of different diameters.

Similar knots:
» pp.105–06
Clove Hitch
» pp.144–45
Double Sheet Bend
» pp.157–59
Fisherman's Knot

Sheer Lashing

- Used for lashing together adjacent poles.
- Also used to reinforce a weak pole.
- Tighten by making two turns across the lashing (frapping turns).
- Start and finish with a Clove Hitch (*see pp.105–06*).
- Ensure the first Clove Hitch is tied around both poles.

1 TIE A CLOVE HITCH (»pp.105–06)

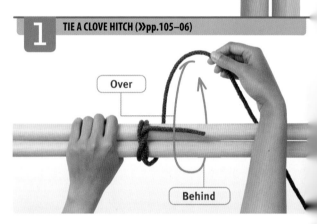

Over

Behind

2

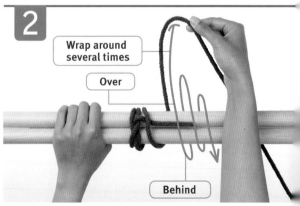

Wrap around several times

Over

Behind

3

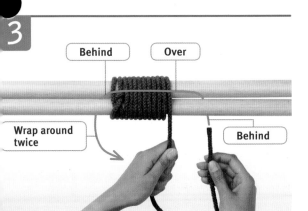

Behind | Over

Wrap around twice

Behind

4

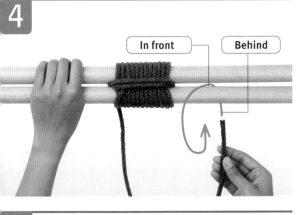

In front | Behind

5

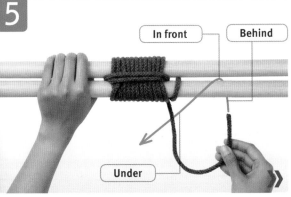

In front | Behind

Under

6

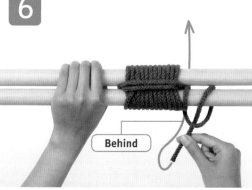

Behind

7

Tighten to finish

A-Frame Lashing

- Follows the same process as a Sheer Lashing (*see pp.222–24*).
- Can be used to form the legs of a rope bridge.
- Make the turns looser, so the poles can be pulled into an "A" shape.

cicle Hitch

More grip than the Rolling Hitch
(see pp.176–77).
Good for use on slippery surfaces.
For additional grip, add extra turns
at the start of the knot.
Ensure that the first series of turns
are locked under the diagonal turn.
For increased security, hold the line
with your hand as strain is applied.

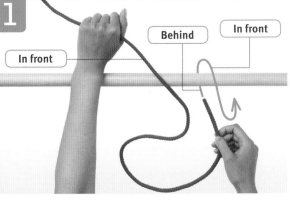

1

In front

Behind | In front

In front

2

Behind | In front

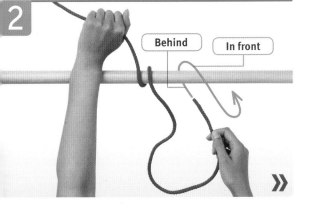

»

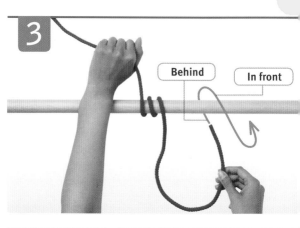

3

Behind | In front

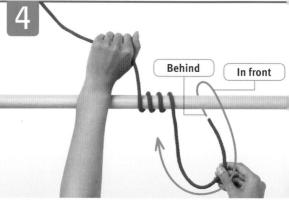

4

Behind | In front

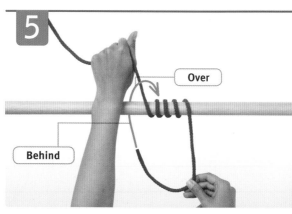

5

Over

Behind

6

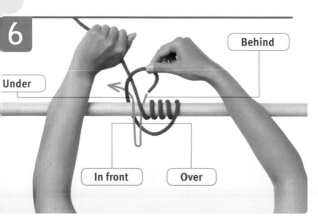

Behind

Under

In front

Over

7

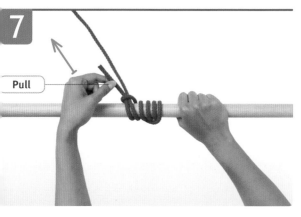

Pull

8

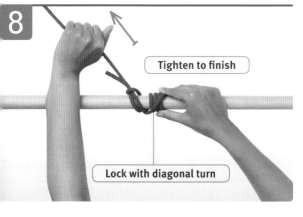

Tighten to finish

Lock with diagonal turn

Prusik Knot

- Used to attach a climbing sling to a main rope.
- Will slide up and down the main rope when strain is removed.
- Sling should be half the diameter of the main rope at most.
- Created in 1931 by Dr Carl Prusik, an Austrian mountaineer.

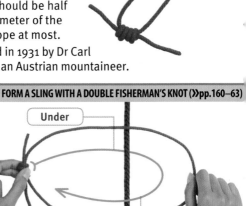

1 FORM A SLING WITH A DOUBLE FISHERMAN'S KNOT (>>pp.160–63)

Under

Over

2

Under

Over

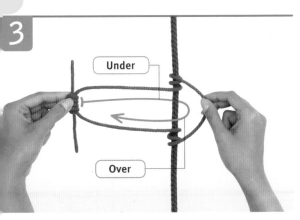

3

Under

Over

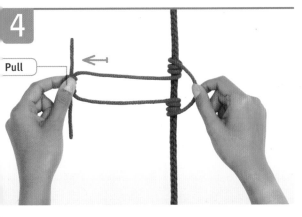

4

Pull

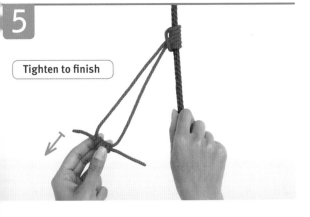

5

Tighten to finish

Bachmann Knot

- Used by climbers to ascend a fixed rope.
- Grips the rope tightly when loaded.
- Strain should only be applied to the sling, not the karabiner.
- Use the karabiner to move up and down the rope when there is no strain on the sling.

1 FORM A SLING WITH A DOUBLE FISHERMAN'S KNOT (»pp.160–63)

Place in karabiner

2

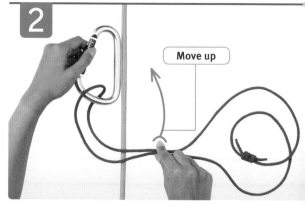

Move up

3

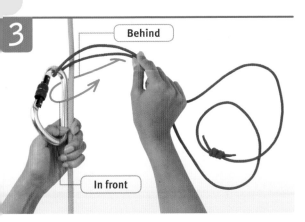

Behind

In front

4

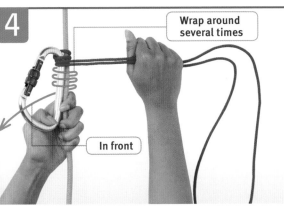

Wrap around
several times

In front

5

Tighten to finish

Klemheist Knot

- A variation of the Prusik Knot (*see pp.228–29*) that can be used for moving up or down a climbing rope.
- Soft tubular climbing tape can be used to form the sling.
- The rope used to form the sling should be at least half the diameter of the main rope.

1 FORM A SLING WITH A DOUBLE FISHERMAN'S KNOT (»pp.160–63)

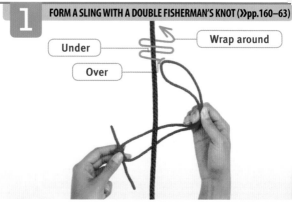

Under
Over
Wrap around

2

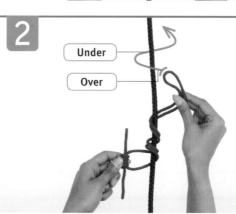

Under
Over

3

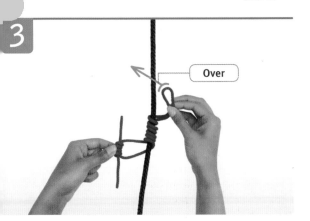

Over

4

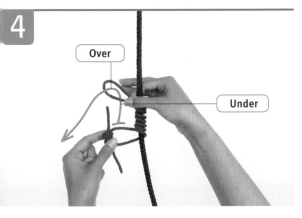

Over

Under

5

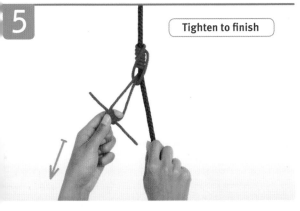

Tighten to finish

Italian Hitch

- A sliding hitch used in climbing and abseiling to control a descent.
- Pull on the loaded rope (rope that takes the strain) to cause the knot to slip.
- Pull on the braking rope to control the speed of the slip.
- The braking rope should not be confused with the loaded rope.

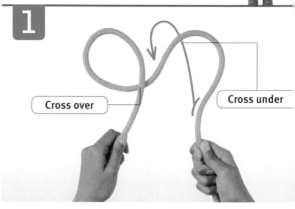

1

Cross over

Cross under

2

Fold over

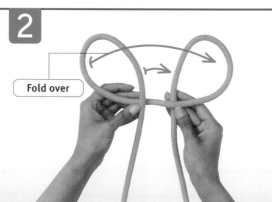

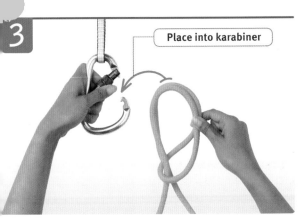

3 Place into karabiner

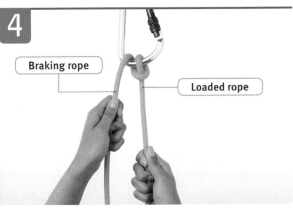

4 Braking rope | Loaded rope

Reversed Italian Hitch

- In the Reversed Italian Hitch, the loaded rope and the braking rope are reversed.

- The braking rope becomes the loaded rope, and vice versa.

Braking rope

Loaded rope

Loops

A loop knot can be used to secure a rope to an object, such as a hook or a ring, or may even be tied around a person's wrist or waist. Loop knots can also be used to join two separate ropes of different thicknesses.

Alpine Butterfly

- Used by climbers to secure themselves to the middle of a rope.
- Will take strain in either direction.
- Can be tied quickly.

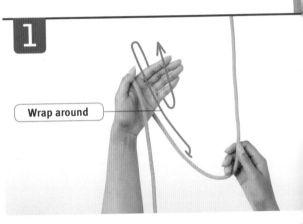

1

Wrap around

2

Over

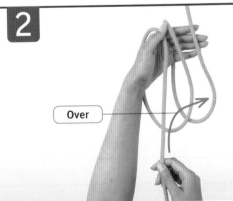

3

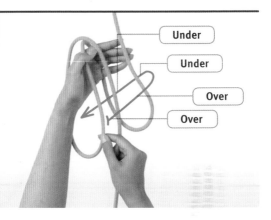

Under

Under

Over

Over

4

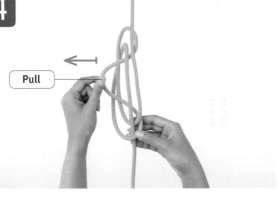

Pull

5

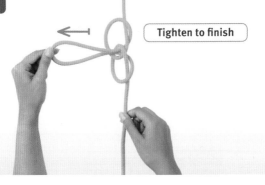

Tighten to finish

Bowline

- A widely used, general-purpose loop knot.
- Easy to tie and untie.
- Ensure that the finished knot has a good tail.
- Can be tied in two ways (*see pp.242–44*) – use this method when the standing part is free.

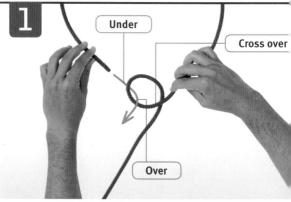

1

Under

Cross over

Over

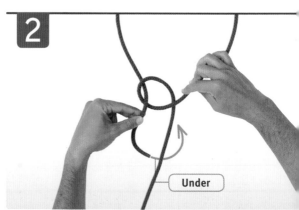

2

Under

3

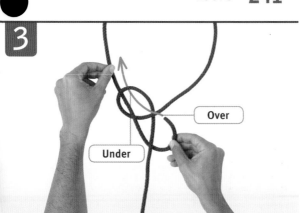

Over

Under

4

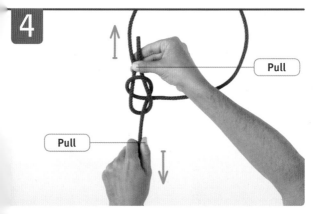

Pull

Pull

5

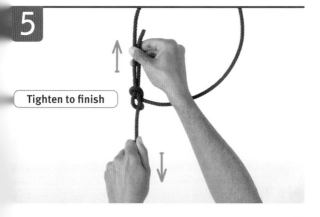

Tighten to finish

Bowline – Second Method

- Used to tie a loop around the waist for activities such as sailing and climbing.
- Ensure that the loop has a good tail (short end).
- Best method for tying a Bowline (*see pp.240–41*) if the standing end of the rope is fixed.

1

Over

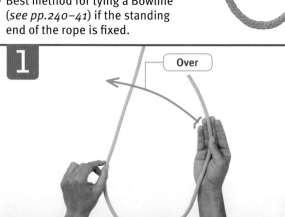

2

Turn palm to face body

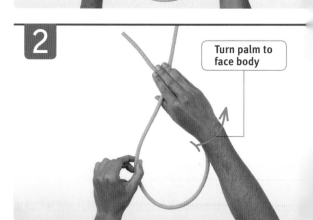

3

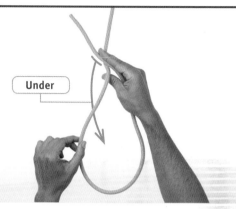

Under

4

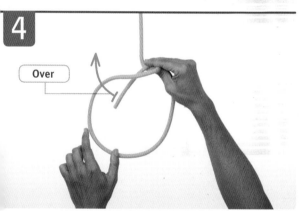

Over

5

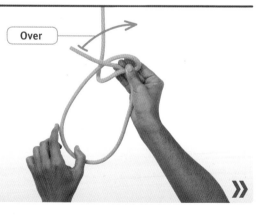

Over

»

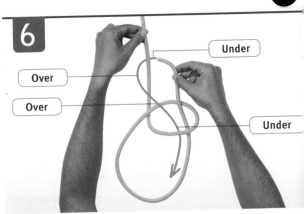

6

Over

Over

Under

Under

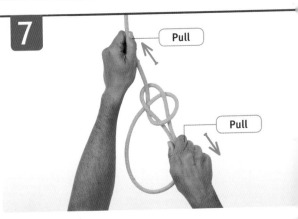

7

Pull

Pull

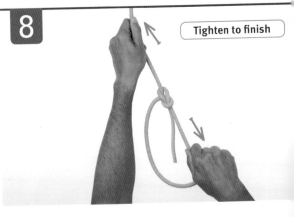

8

Tighten to finish

Bowline with Two Turns

A more secure version of a Bowline (*see pp.240–43*) tied with an extra turn. Ensure the finished knot has a good tail (working end).

1

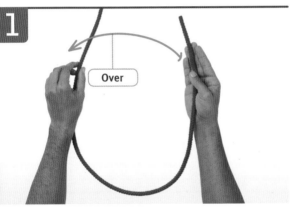

Over

2

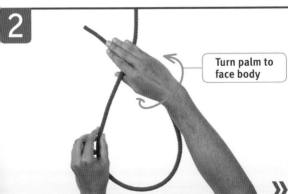

Turn palm to face body

»

3

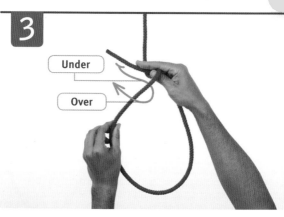

Under

Over

4

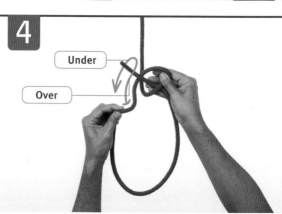

Under

Over

5

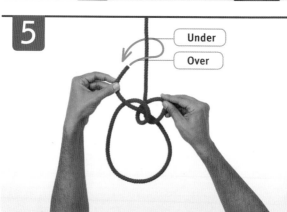

Under

Over

6

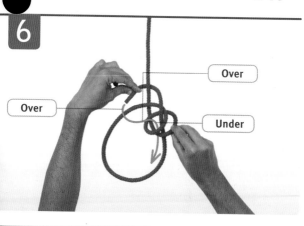

Over

Over

Under

7

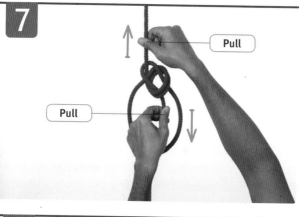

Pull

Pull

8

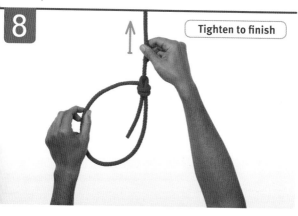

Tighten to finish

Bowline with Stopper

- A secure version of the Bowline (*see pp.240–43*) that is popular with climbers.
- Working end is tied around the loop using the Overhand Knot (*see pp.28–29*).

1 | TIE A BOWLINE (»pp.240–43)

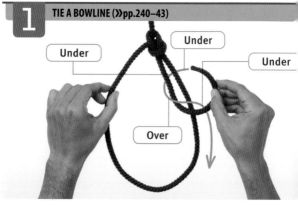

Under

Under

Under

Over

2

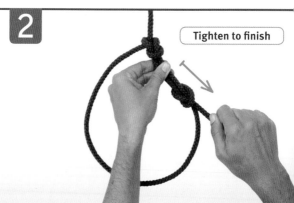

Tighten to finish

Figure-of-Eight Loop

- A popular climber's loop that can take a moderate amount of strain.
- Distinctive shape makes it easy to check if the knot is secure.
- Can be tied in fine nylon.
- Also known as the Double Figure-of-Eight Knot.

1

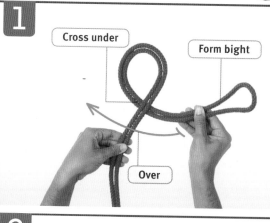

Cross under

Form bight

Over

2

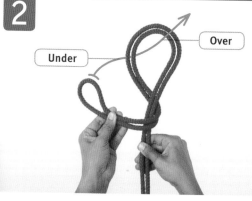

Under

Over

≫

3

Pull

4

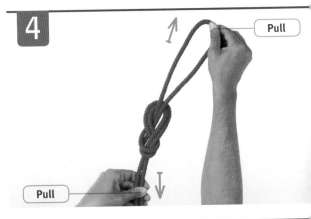

Pull

Pull

5

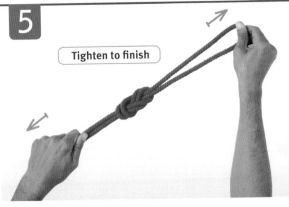

Tighten to finish

Threaded Figure-of-Eight Loop

A Figure-of-Eight Loop (*see pp.249–50*) that can be threaded through a ring, Used for attaching climbing rope to a harness.

The finished knot should be neat and snug.

Not as easy to untie as the Bowline (*see pp.240–41*).

1 TIE A FIGURE OF EIGHT (»pp.38–39)

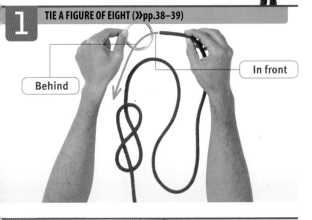

Behind

In front

2

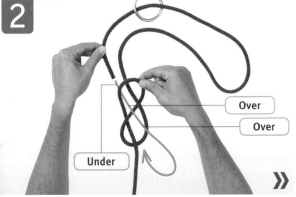

Over

Over

Under

»

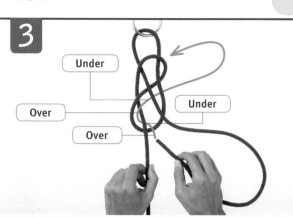

3

Under

Over

Under

Over

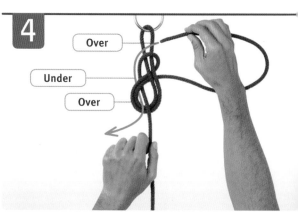

4

Over

Under

Over

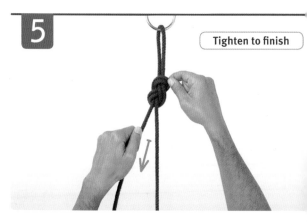

5

Tighten to finish

Overhand Loop

A simple method for
creating a fixed loop.
Made from an Overhand Knot
(see pp.28–29) tied in the bight.
Difficult to untie.

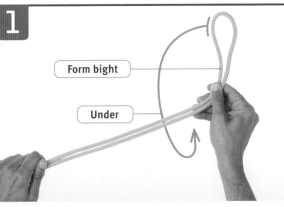

1

Form bight

Under

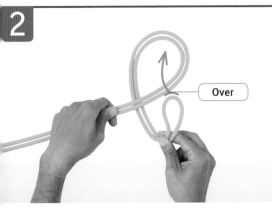

2

Over

»

3

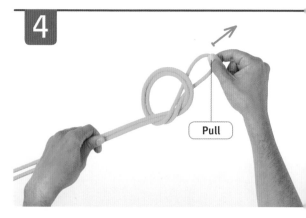

Under

4

Pull

5

Tighten to finish

Double Overhand Loop

loop knot suitable for all types of thin
opes and cords, such as fishing line.
ied using the same method as the Double
Overhand Knot (*see pp.32–33*), but with a
oubled length of rope.

an be difficult to untie.

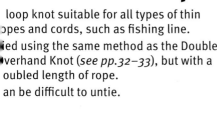

1

Form bight

Under

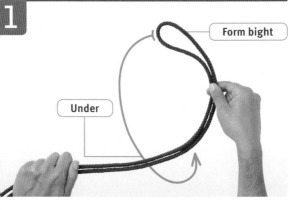

2

Under

Over

»

3

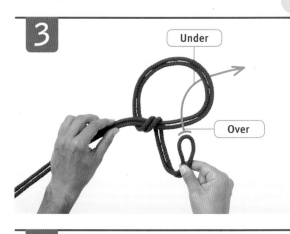

Under

Over

4

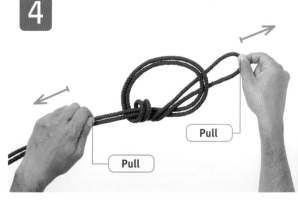

Pull

Pull

5

Tighten to finish

Double Overhand Sliding Loop

Good for attaching a fishing line to a hook or a cord to a pair of spectacles. Work the knot into a neat shape to ensure it slides easily.

1

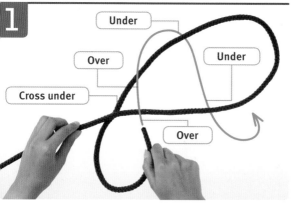

Under

Under

Over

Cross under

Over

2

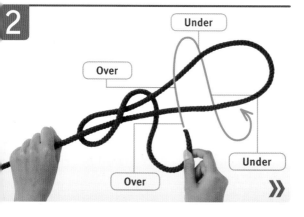

Under

Over

Under

Over

»

3

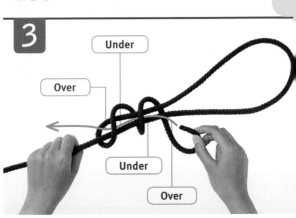

Under

Over

Under

Over

4

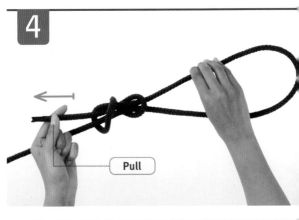

Pull

5

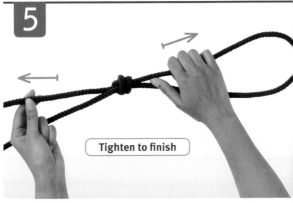

Tighten to finish

Bowline on the Bight

A secure, double loop knot that can take strain.

Each of the two fixed loops can be used for separate functions.

Quick to tie and easy to untie.

Can be tied in the middle of the rope.

1

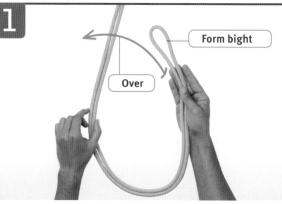

Form bight

Over

2

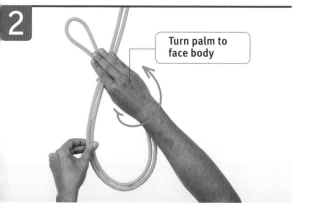

Turn palm to face body

3

Under

Over

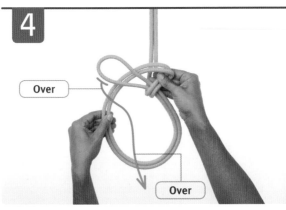

4

Over

Over

5

Over

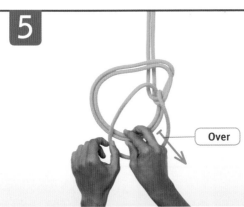

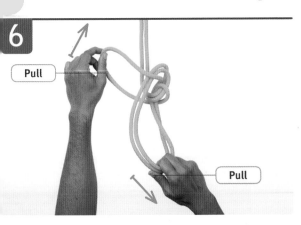

6

Pull

Pull

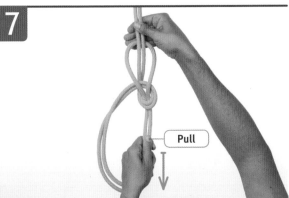

7

Pull

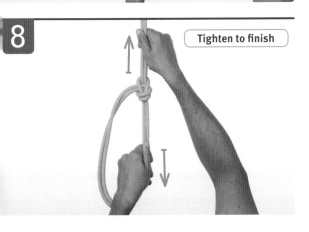

8

Tighten to finish

Portuguese Bowline

- Used to tie two adjustable loops quickly.
- Equal strain must be placed on both loops to prevent them from changing size while in use.

1

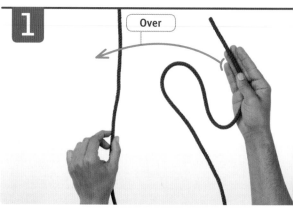

Over

2

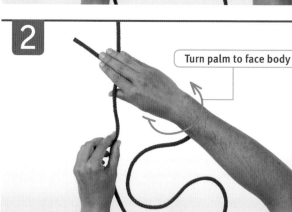

Turn palm to face body

3

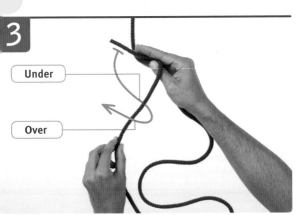

Under

Over

4

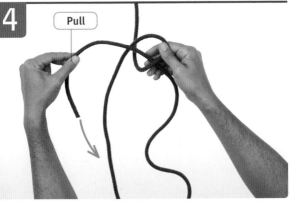

Pull

5

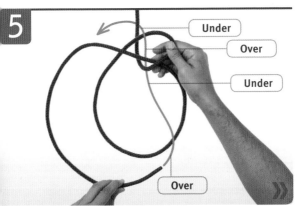

Under

Over

Under

Over

6

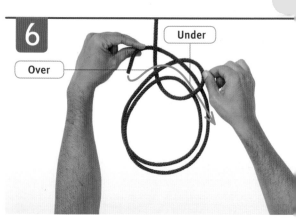

Over

Under

7

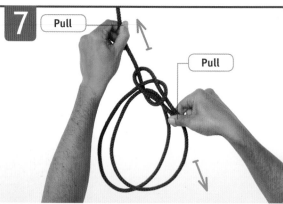

Pull

Pull

8

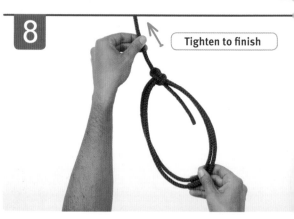

Tighten to finish

Spanish Bowline

A variation of the Bowline (*see pp.240–43*), this knot forms two adjustable loops that lock into position.

Can be tied in the middle of the rope.

Place equal strain on both loops.

1

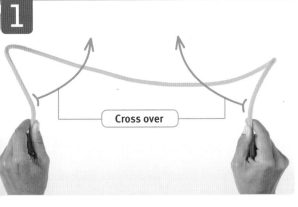

Cross over

2

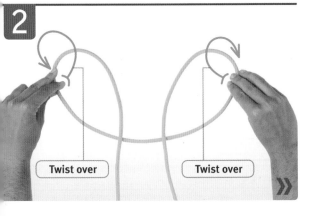

Twist over

Twist over

3

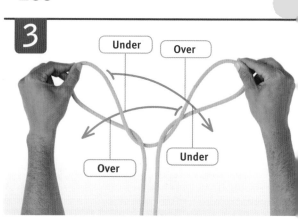

Under · Over · Over · Under

4

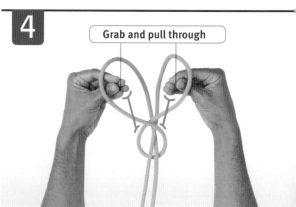

Grab and pull through

5

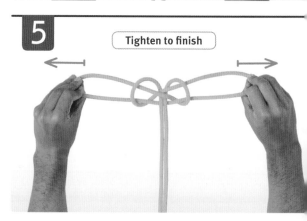

Tighten to finish

ngler's Loop

deal for making a fixed loop
n thin lines and ropes.

Also works well with elasticated
cord (shock cord).

Quick to tie.

Not suitable for thick ropes as it
can be difficult to untie.

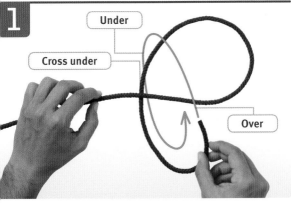

1 Under | Cross under | Over

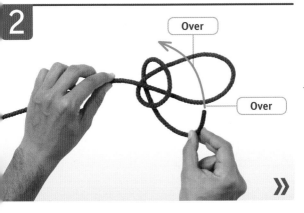

2 Over | Over

»

3

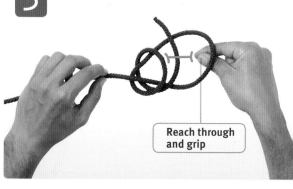

Reach through and grip

4

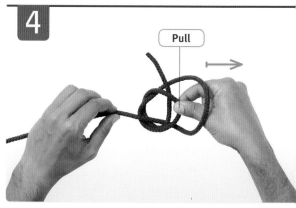

Pull

5

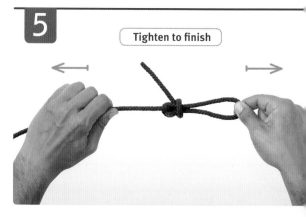

Tighten to finish

Single Figure-of-Eight Loop on the Bight

Can be tied in the middle of the rope.
Quick to tie and reasonably easy to untie.
Creates a loop that can only be pulled in one direction.

1

Over

Form bight

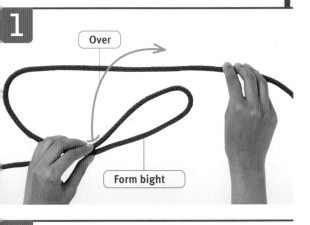

2

Under

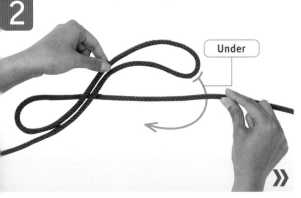

»

3

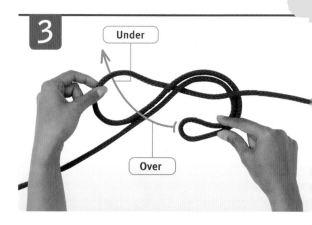

Under

Over

4

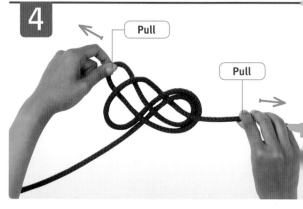

Pull

Pull

5

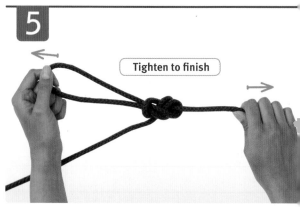

Tighten to finish

Englishman's Loop

Used to form a fixed loop.
Based on two Overhand Knots
(see pp.28–29).
Similar to the Fisherman's Knot
(see pp.157–59).

1

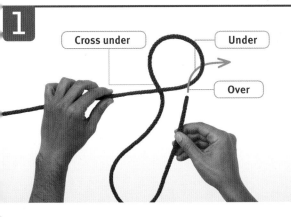

Cross under | Under

Over

2

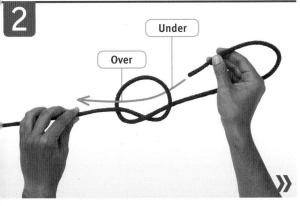

Under

Over

》

3

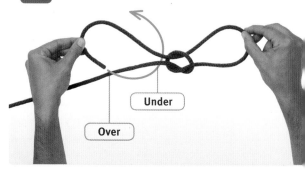

4

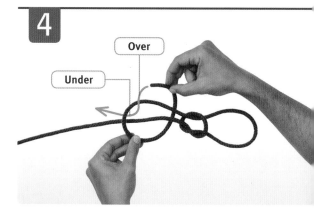

5

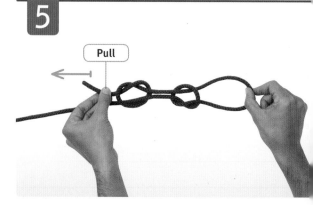

6

Bring knots together

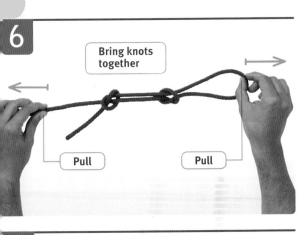

Pull

Pull

7

Tighten to finish

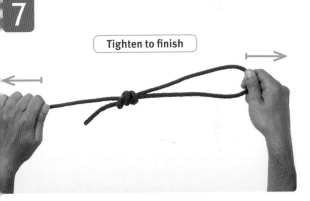

Double Englishman's Loop

- Provides extra security when used with a very slippery line.
- Simply double each Overhand Knot (see pp.28–29) tied in the Englishman's Loop (see pp.271–73).
- Use only in thin line and cords.

BEST FOR ...
fishing

Being able to secure a line to a hook is a fundamental angling skill. It is important to remember that some fishing knots can only be used with lines of a certain thickness and material.

Palomar Knot
pp.209–10

✓ The strongest knot for tying a fishing line to a hook –can take a great deal of strain.

✓ Will work with even the most slippery nylon line.

✓ Moistening the line will give a neater finish to the knot.

Similar knots:
**》 pp.205–06
Snelling a Hook
》 pp.207–08
Clinch Knot**

Blood Knot
pp.168–71

✓ Commonly used by anglers to join together two thin pieces of nylon line.

✓ Can take a great deal of strain.

✓ Moistening the line will help to draw the knot tight.

Similar knots:
**》 pp.157–59
Fisherman's Knot
》 pp.160–63 Double
Fisherman's Knot**

Figure-of-Eight Loop » pp.249–50

✅ A knot that is quick to tie – even with the finest fishing line.

✅ Favoured by anglers because it is easy to tie and extremely strong.

❌ Difficult to untie, especially when wet.

Similar knots:
» pp.253–5
Overhand L‹
» pp.255–5
Double Overhand Loop

Snelling a Hook » pp.205–06

✅ A strong, neat method for tying line to a hook.

✅ Works on spade-ended hooks (hooks without an eye) as well as eyed hooks.

✅ Moistening the line will help to draw the knot tight.

Similar knots
» p.207–08
Clinch Knot
» p.208
Improved Clinch Knot

lood Dropper Knot
pp.278–79

A loop that allows another lure or bait to be added with a short length of line.

The loop is angled away from the line, helping to prevent tangles.

Similar knots:
**» pp.160–63
Double
Fisherman's
Knot
» p.168–71
Blood Knot**

imini Twist » pp.280–82

A knot that makes a long strong loop in all types fishing line.

Will not slip if it has been tied correctly.

Needs two people and a good deal of practice make successfully.

Similar knots:
**» pp.255–58
Double
Overhand Loop
» pp.269–70 Single
Figure-of-Eight
Loop on the Bight**

Blood Dropper Knot

- Makes a loop at the side of a line for attaching a fishing fly or lure.
- Tied at the end of the line.
- Moisten line to help draw the knot tight.

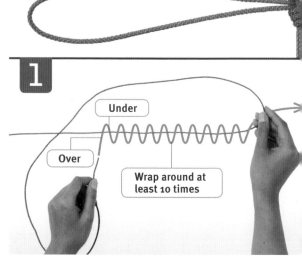

1

Under

Over

Wrap around at least 10 times

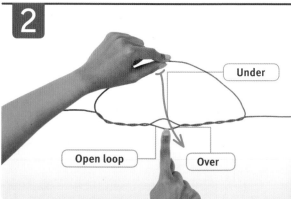

2

Under

Open loop

Over

3

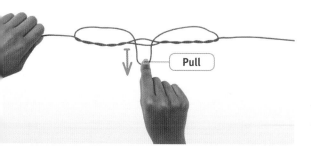

Pull

4

Pull

Pull

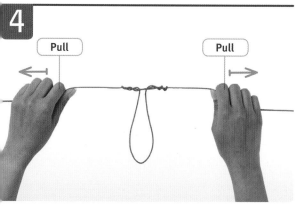

5

Tighten to finish

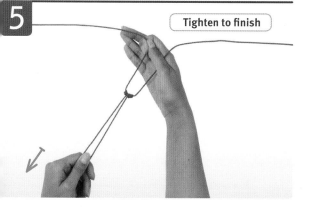

Bimini Twist

- Originally developed for use in big-game fishing.
- Suitable for both braided and monofilament fishing line.
- Forms a long, strong loop at the end of a fishing line.
- Needs practice and more than one person to tie.

1 Double the line

Twist hand clockwise

2

Open loop

3

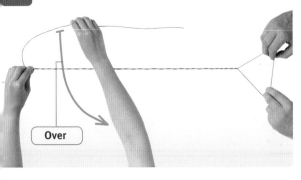

Over

4

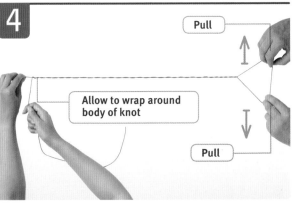

Pull

Allow to wrap around body of knot

Pull

5

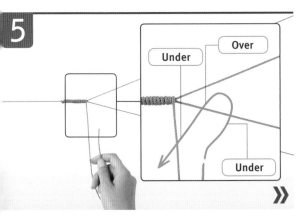

Over

Under

Under

»

6

Pull

7

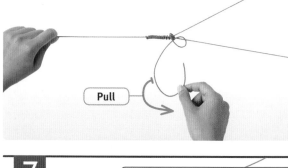

Wrap around

Over

Under

Under

8

Tighten and trim to finish

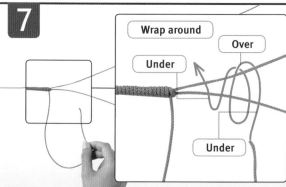

Basic Net

A widely used technique for making and mending nets.

Use a netting needle (*see p.19, p.284*) to hold the line while you work.

Use a gauge – a piece of wood roughly half the diameter of the mesh – to ensure even spacing.

1 TIE CLOVE HITCHES (»pp.140–41) AROUND A POLE

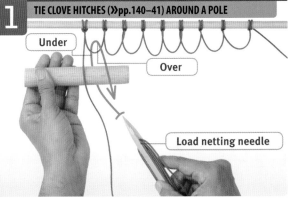

Under

Over

Load netting needle

2

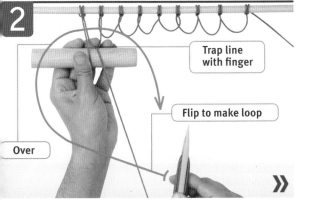

Trap line with finger

Flip to make loop

Over

»

3

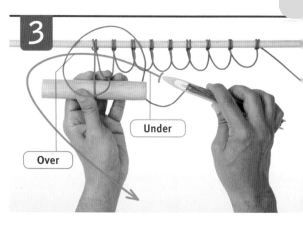

Under

Over

4

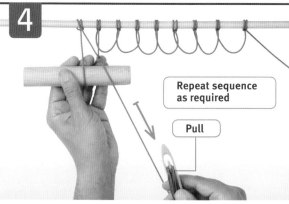

Repeat sequence as required

Pull

Loading a needle

- Tie a half hitch with the line around the spike in the middle of the needle.

- Pass the long end of the line under the needle and back up the other side.

- Loop the line around the spike and back under the needle; repeat until finished.

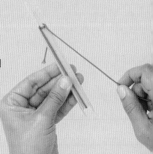

Cargo Net Knot

Used to make a square net from heavy rope. Tied with one long rope and one shorter rope. Lay the long rope vertically and the short rope horizontally.

1

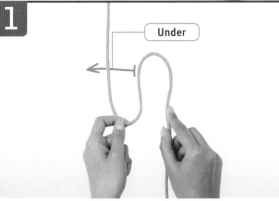

Under

2

Under

Under

Over

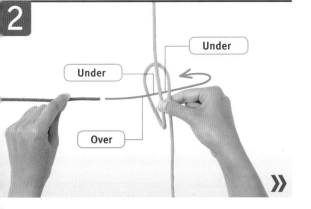

»

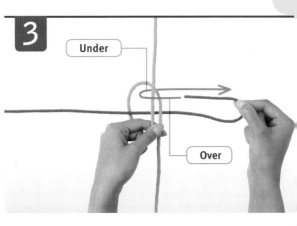

3

Under

Over

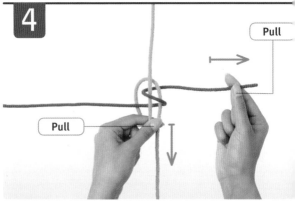

4

Pull

Pull

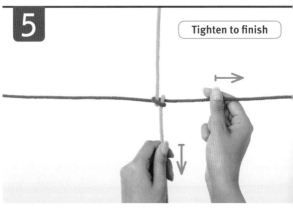

5

Tighten to finish

ry Mast Knot

A simple technique or tying a multiple oop knot.

Not suitable for use in thick rope.

Can be difficult to untie.

1

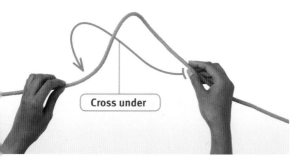

Cross under

2

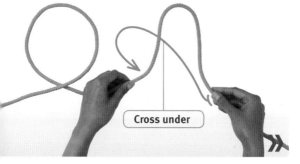

Cross under

3

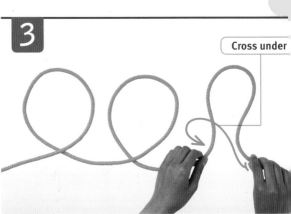

Cross under

4

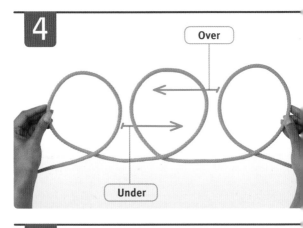

Over

Under

5

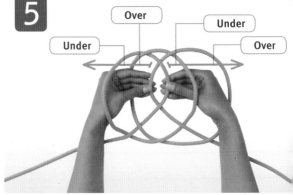

Over

Under

Under

Over

6

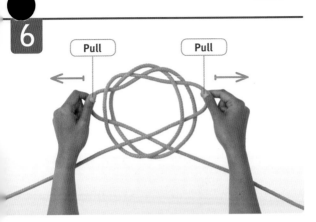

Pull

Pull

7

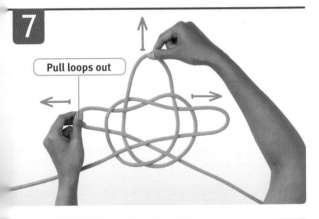

Pull loops out

8

Tidy to finish

Plaits and Sennits

A plait is used to interweave strands of rope or fine line into an arrangement that is both strong and decorative. Complex weaves of strands are known as sennits.

Three-Strand Flat Plait

- The simplest of plaits.
- Bind one end of the strands together (*see pp.374–75*) before starting.
- Move alternate outer strands to the middle of the plait.
- Keep all the strands flat and tight as you plait.

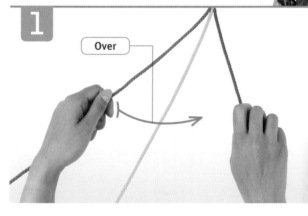

1

Over

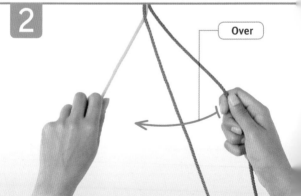

2

Over

3

Over

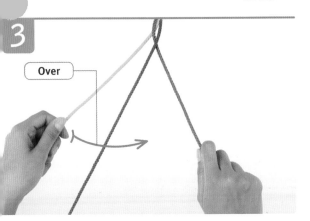

4

Repeat sequence as required

Over

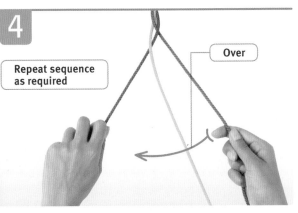

5 WHIP (>>pp.374-75) STRANDS TOGETHER TO FINISH

Four-Strand Flat Plait

- Forms an asymmetric flat plait.
- More decorative than the Three-Strand Flat Plait (*see pp.292–93*).
- Bind one end of the strands together (*see pp.374–75*) before starting.
- Keep all the strands flat and tight as you plait.

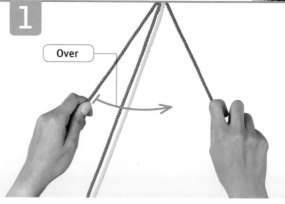

Over

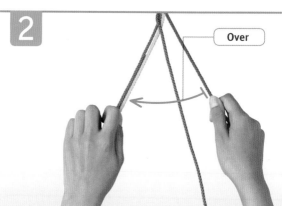

Over

3

Over

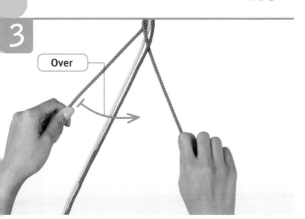

4

Repeat sequence as required

Over

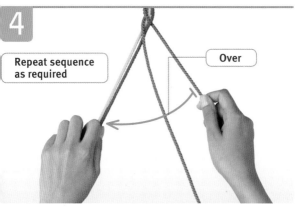

5 WHIP (»pp.374–75) STRANDS TOGETHER TO FINISH

Five-Strand Flat Plait

- Move alternate outer strands to the middle of the plait.
- Bind one end of the strands together (*see pp.374–75*) before starting.
- Keep all the strands flat and tight as you plait.

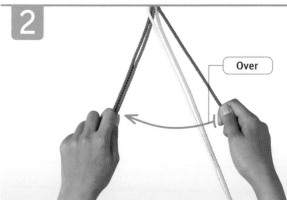

1

Over

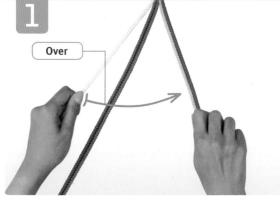

2

Over

3

Over

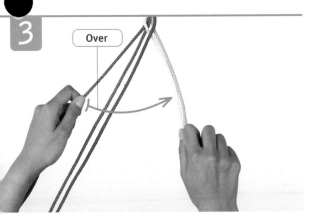

4

Repeat sequence as required

Over

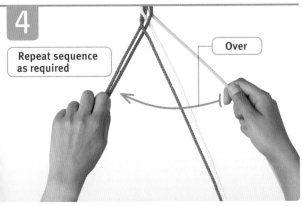

5 WHIP (»pp.374–75) STRANDS TOGETHER TO FINISH

Six-Strand Flat Plait

- Forms a large, asymmetrical decorative plait.
- Bind one end of the strands together (*see pp. 374–75*) before starting.
- Keep all the strands flat and tight as you plait.

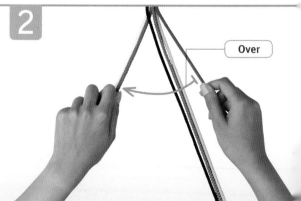

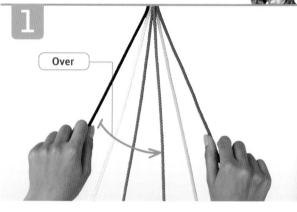

1

Over

2

Over

3

Over

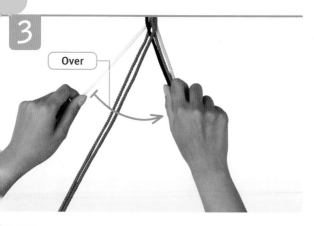

4

Repeat sequence as required

Over

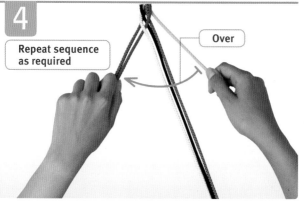

5 WHIP (>>pp.374–75) STRANDS TOGETHER TO FINISH

Seven-Strand Flat Plait

- Used to form a large decorative plait.
- The largest number of strands with which it is practical to make a plait.
- Bind one end of the strands together (*see pp.374–75*) before starting.
- Keep all the strands flat and tight as you plait.

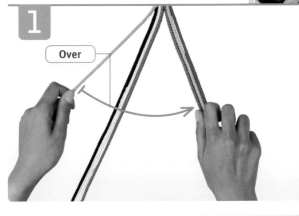

1

Over

2

Over

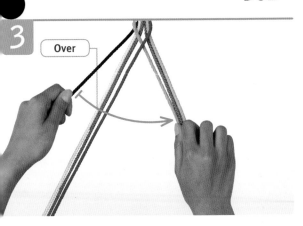

3

Over

4

Repeat sequence as required

Over

5 WHIP (≫pp.374–75) STRANDS TOGETHER TO FINISH

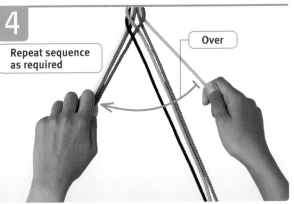

BEST FOR ...
Gifts

here are a number of knots that are decorative
s well as practical. They are ideal for making
ttractive and useful gifts.

Monkey's Fist » pp.49–53

✓ A decorative ball knot that is
perfect for making a key fob.
eize (*see pp.387–89*) a loop on
ne end to attach the keys.

Similar knots:
**» pp.62–71
Manrope Knot**

✓ Can also be turned into
a doorstop –simply
e the knot with large
ope, and place a weight
n its centre.

Basic Net » pp.283–84

✓ Used to make a
durable, lasting net.

✓ The finished net can
be as large or small
s you want, and may be
sed for storage or even
s part of a hammock.

✗ Requires the use of a
netting needle (*see p.19*).

Similar
knots:
**» pp.285–86
Cargo Net
Knot**

True Lover's Knot
» pp.80–81

☑ One of many knots used as as a symbol of binding love between two people.

☑ Can be mounted in a frame to make a wedding present.

☑ The two Overhand Knots (*see pp.28–29*) are separate but interlinked.

Similar knots:
» pp.82–84
Sailor's Cross

Square Crown Sennit » pp.330–31

✓ Easily made into a bracelet or belt.

✓ Highly decorative, but relatively simple to make.

✓ A core can be added to the centre of the sennit to create a key fob.

Similar knots:
» pp.327–29
Six-Strand Round Crowning

Turk's Head – Four-Lead Five-Bight
pp.128–32

✓ Can be used to make a decorative napkin ring.

✓ Can also be flattened to make a small mat or coaster.

✓ The knot's structure can be stiffened by covering the inside of it with PVA glue.

Similar knots:
» pp.117–23
Turk's Head – Three-Lead Four-Bight

Oval Mat » pp.311–15

✓ Can be used to make a coaster, table mat, or doormat.

✓ Thinner rope is best for a coaster or table mat, thicker rope for a doormat.

✓ The pattern can be doubled or tripled, as required.

Similar knots:
» pp.306–10
Ocean-Plait Mat

Ocean-Plait Mat

- Used to make a decorative mat.
- Tie loosely before working into a neat, taut final shape.
- Follow the pattern around two, three, four, or even five times to make a larger mat.

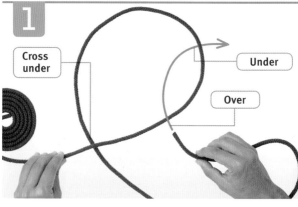

1

Cross under

Under

Over

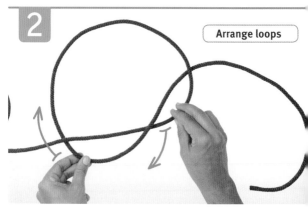

2

Arrange loops

3

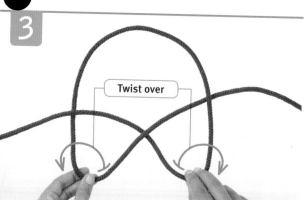

Twist over

4

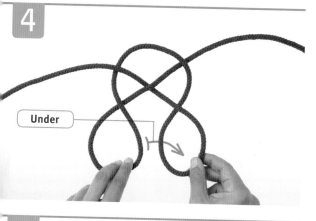

Under

5

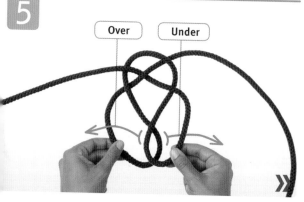

Over   Under

6 Make crossed strands even

7

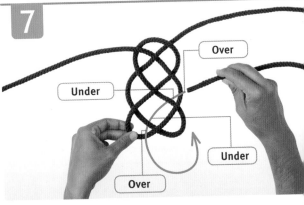

Under

Over

Under

Over

8 Make crossed strands even

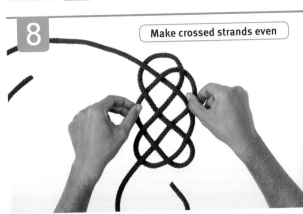

9

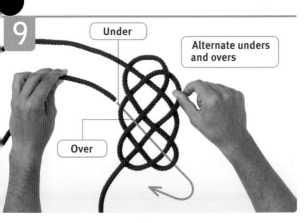

Under

Alternate unders
and overs

Over

10

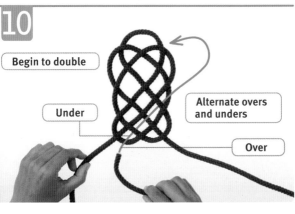

Begin to double

Under

Alternate overs
and unders

Over

11

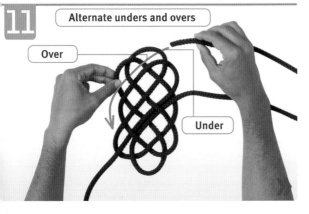

Alternate unders and overs

Over

Under

12

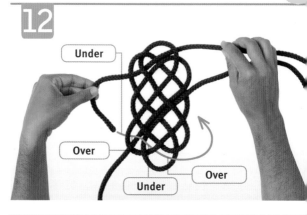

Under

Over

Under

Over

13

Alternate unders and overs

Over

Under

14

Follow around again or trim and tuck to finish

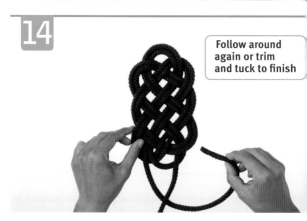

Oval Mat

Used to make a
decorative mat.

Use thin rope for
a table mat and thick
rope for a doormat.

Pattern can be
followed around
three or more times.

Requires a large
amount of rope.

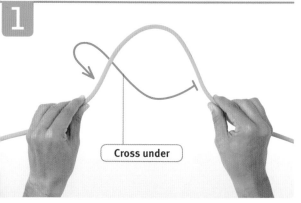

Cross under

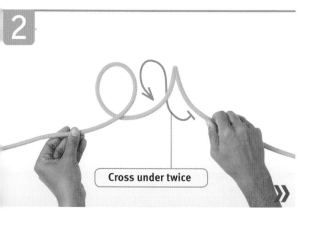

Cross under twice

3

Under | Over

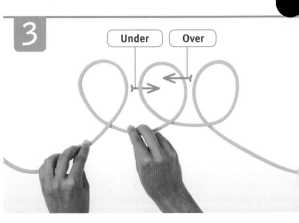

4

Over

Under

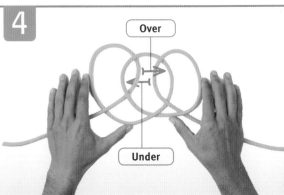

5

Arrange crossing turns

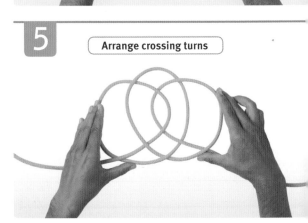

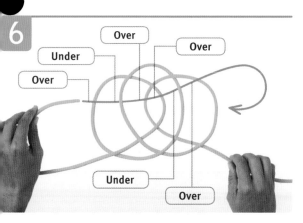

6

Over

Over

Under

Over

Under

Over

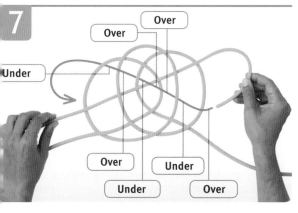

7

Over

Over

Under

Over

Under

Under

Over

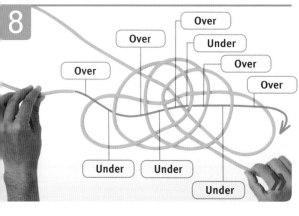

8

Over

Over

Under

Over

Over

Under

Under

Under

9

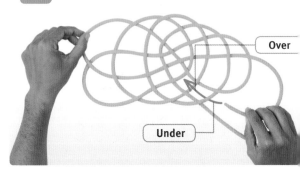

Over

Under

10

Start to double with long end, alternating overs and unders

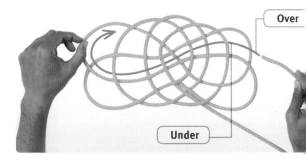

Over

Under

11

Over

Under

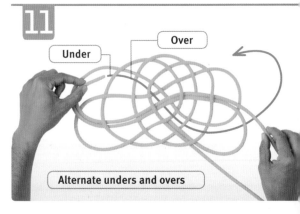

Alternate unders and overs

12

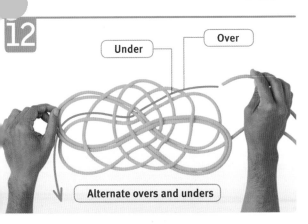

Under

Over

Alternate overs and unders

13

Alternate overs and unders

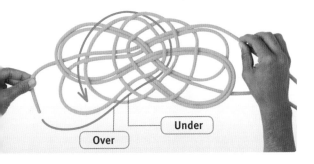

Over

Under

14

Follow around again or
trim and tuck to finish

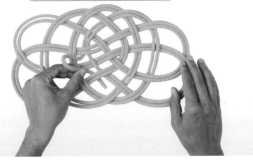

Chain Sennit

- Forms interlinked loops to shorten a rope.
- Also used by climbers to prevent rope from getting tangled.
- Work tight before moving on to the next step.
- Also known as the Drummer's Plait.

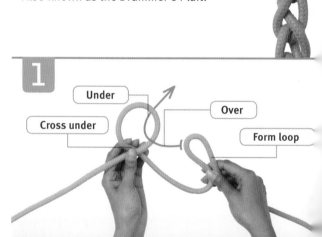

1

Cross under | Under | Over | Form loop

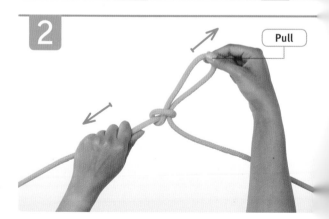

2

Pull

3

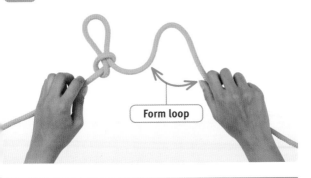

Form loop

4

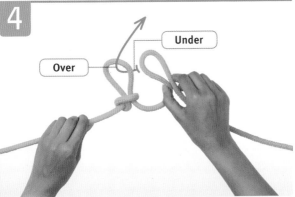

Over

Under

5

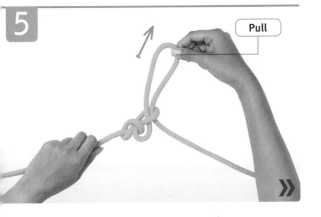

Pull

6

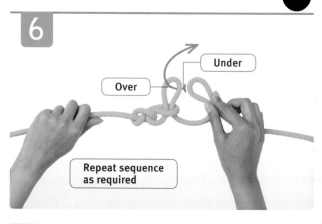

Over — Under

Repeat sequence as required

7

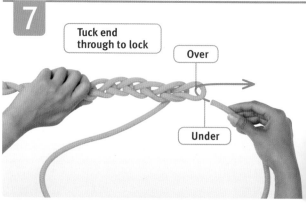

Tuck end through to lock

Over

Under

8

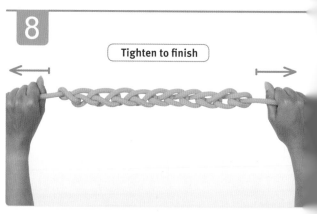

Tighten to finish

Four-Strand Round Sennit

- The simplest of the round plaits.
- Bind one end of the strands together (*see pp.374–75*) before starting.
- Keep all the strands tight as you plait.
- Ensure that you untangle the working ends regularly.

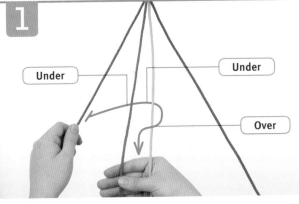

1

Under

Under

Over

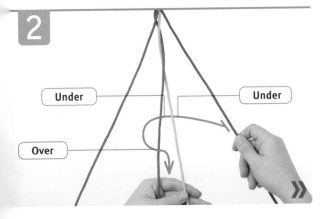

2

Under

Under

Over

3

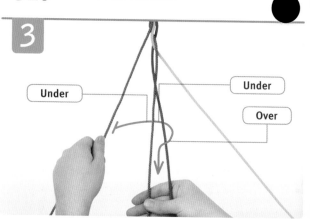

Under

Under

Over

4

Repeat sequence as required

Under

Under

Over

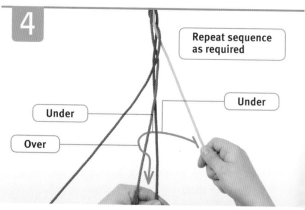

5

WHIP (»pp.374–75) STRANDS TOGETHER TO FINISH

Eight-Strand Square Sennit

A highly decorative sennit.

Bind one end of the strands together (*see pp.374–75*) before starting.

Move alternate outer strands to the middle of the plait.

If you stop while tying, ensure that you start at the correct point in the sequence.

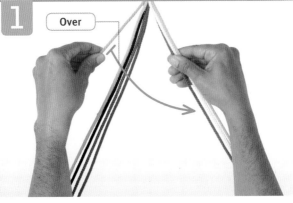

1 Over

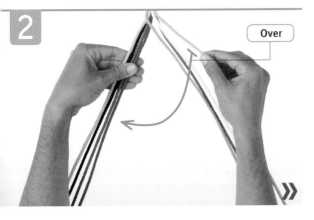

2 Over

»

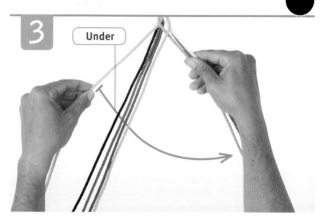

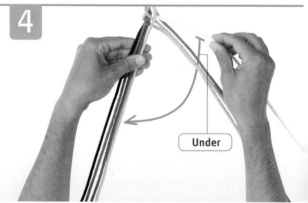

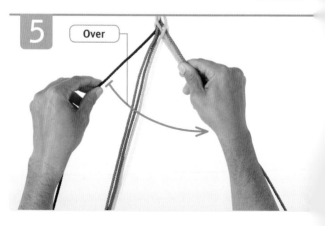

6

Over

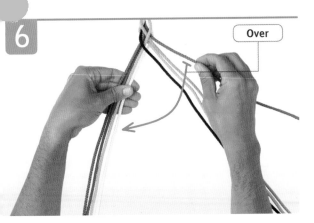

7

Under

Repeat sequence as required

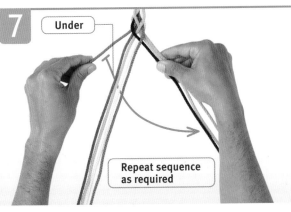

8 WHIP (»pp.374–75) STRANDS TOGETHER TO FINISH

Round Crown Sennit

- Used to convert lengths of line into an attractive, solid braid.
- Formed from a series of Crown Knots (*see pp.54–55*) tied one on top of another.
- Bind one end of the strands together (*see pp.374–75*) before starting.

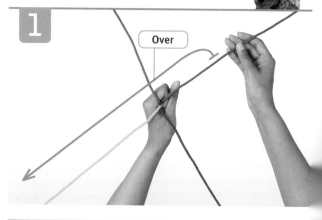

1

Over

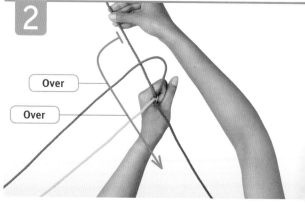

2

Over

Over

3

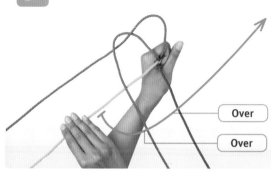

Over

Over

4

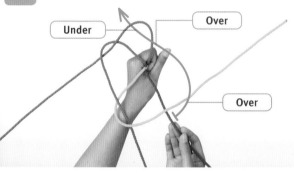

Under

Over

Over

5

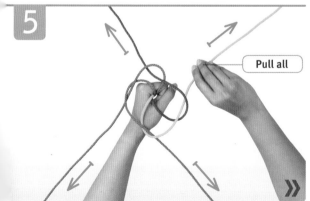

Pull all

»

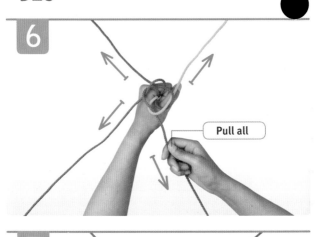

Pull all

Repeat sequence as required

Round Crown Sennit – Four Pairs

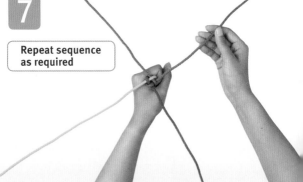

- Uses pairs of line instead of single strands to make a bulkier sennit.
- Follows the same pattern as the Round Crown Sennit (*see pp.324–26*).

Six-Strand Round Crowning

Used to form a cylindrical tube from a sennit.
Made by tying a series of Crown Knots (see pp.54–55).
Bind one end of the strands together (see pp.374–75) before starting.
Not suitable for use in large-diameter rope.

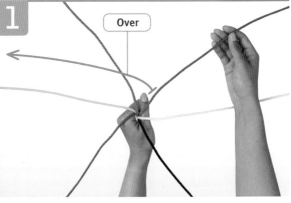

1 Over

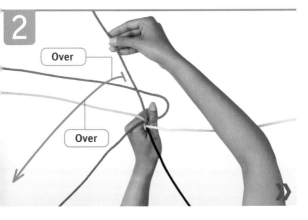

2 Over

Over

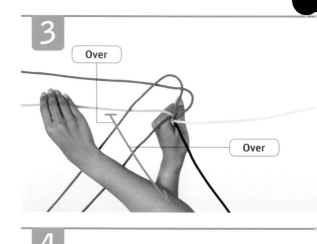

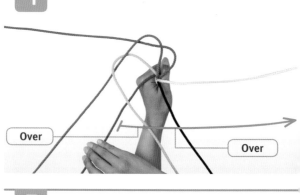

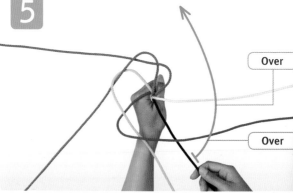

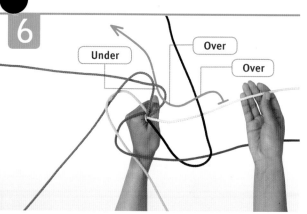

6

Under
Over
Over

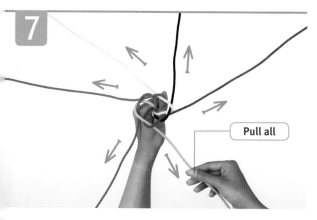

7

Pull all

8

Repeat sequence as required

Square Crown Sennit

- A decorative knot used in cords and bracelets.
- Formed from Crown Knots (*see pp.54–55*) tied in alternate directions.
- Bind one end of the strands together (*see pp.374–75*) before starting.
- Tighten each Crown Knot before moving to the next stage.

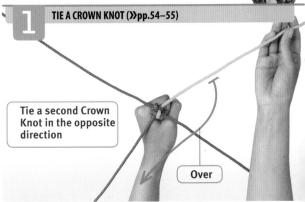

1   TIE A CROWN KNOT (>>pp.54–55)

Tie a second Crown Knot in the opposite direction

Over

2

Over

Over

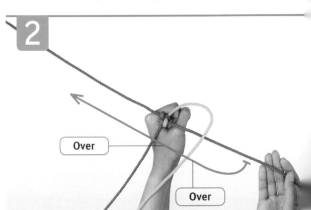

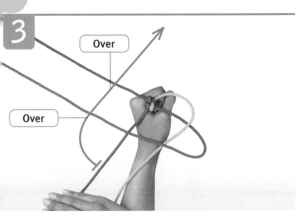

3

Over

Over

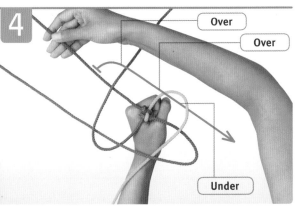

4

Over

Over

Under

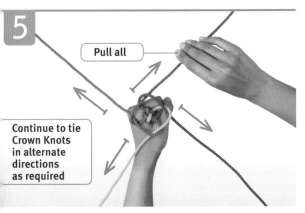

5

Pull all

Continue to tie
Crown Knots
in alternate
directions
as required

Splices and Whippings

A splice is a permanent way of finishing a rope using its strands or of joining together two ropes of equal width. A whipping is tied at the end of a rope and prevents it from coming undone.

Back Splice

- Used as a permanent finish to the end of a rope.
- Increases the diameter of a rope end by one-third.
- Before you start tie a Crown Knot (*see pp.54–55*) with the strands, leaving long strand ends.
- Whip (*see pp.374–75*) or tape the working ends to make the strands easier to tuck.

1 **TIE A CROWN KNOT (》pp.54–55)**

Insert Swedish fid

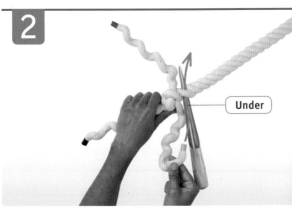

2

Under

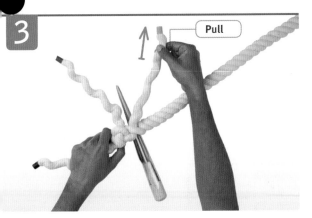

3 Pull

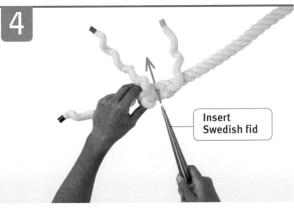

4 Insert Swedish fid

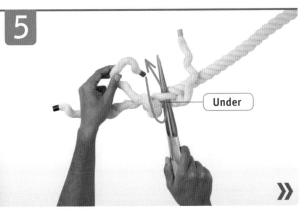

5 Under

»

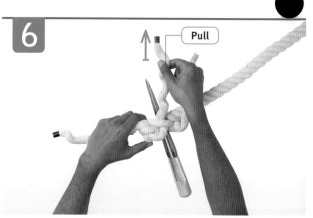

6 Pull

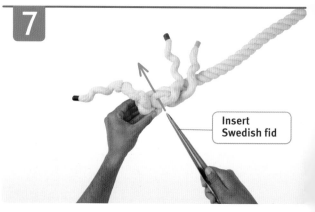

7 Insert Swedish fid

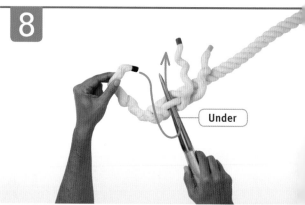

8 Under

9

Pull

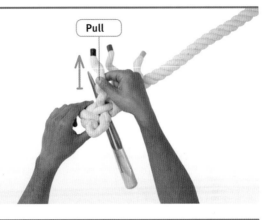

10

Arrange strands

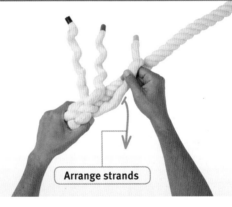

11

Begin a second cycle of tucks

Insert Swedish fid

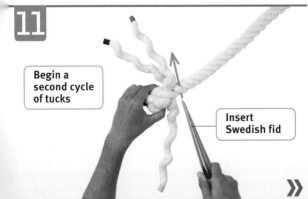

»

12

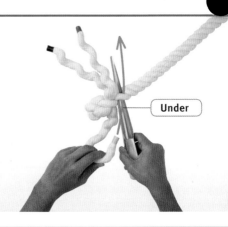

Under

13

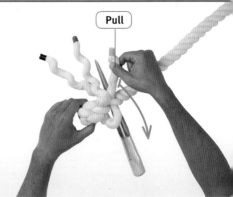

Pull

14

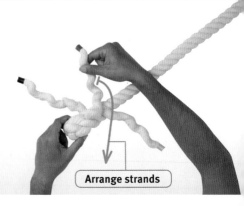

Arrange strands

15

Insert
Swedish fid

16

Under

17

Pull

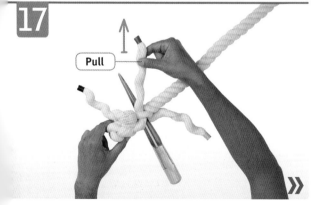

»

18

Arrange strands

19

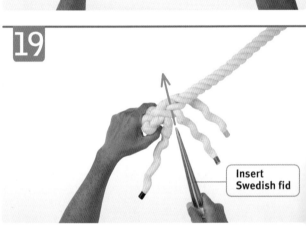

Insert Swedish fid

20

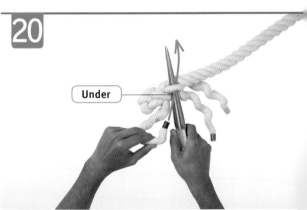

Under

21

Pull

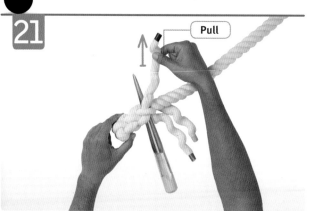

22

Make a final
cycle of tucks

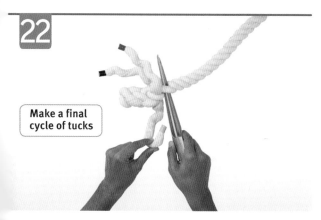

23

Trim to finish

Eye Splice

- Forms a permanent loop at the end of a three-strand rope.
- Ensure a tight start to the splice.
- Make a minimum of three full tucks for a natural fibre rope and five tucks for synthetic rope, as it is more slippery.

1

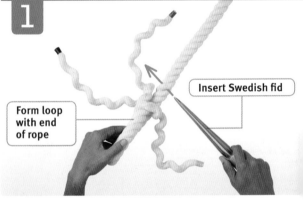

Form loop with end of rope

Insert Swedish fid

2

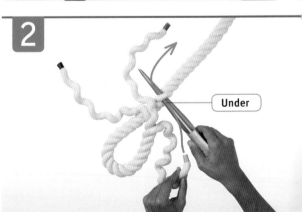

Under

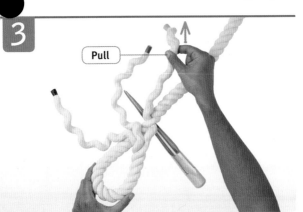

3

Pull

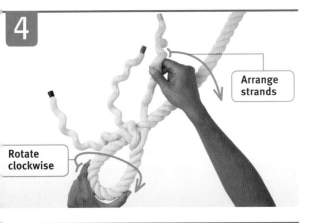

4

Arrange strands

Rotate clockwise

5

Under

»

6

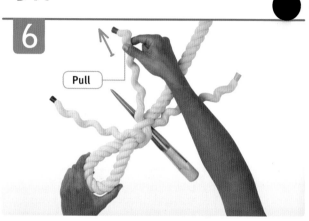

Pull

7

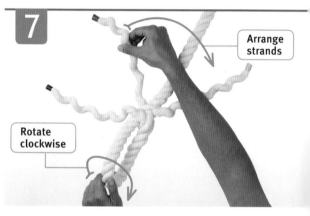

Arrange strands

Rotate clockwise

8

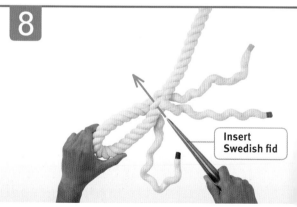

Insert Swedish fid

9

Under

10

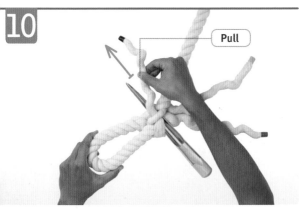

Pull

11

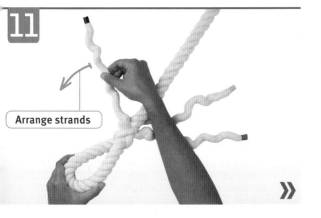

Arrange strands

»

12

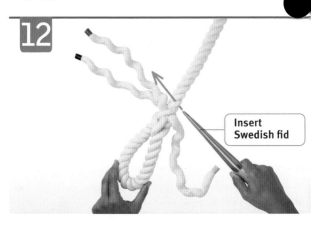

Insert Swedish fid

13

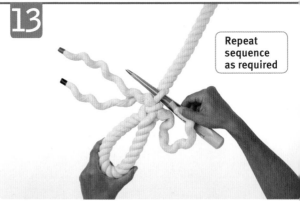

Repeat sequence as required

14

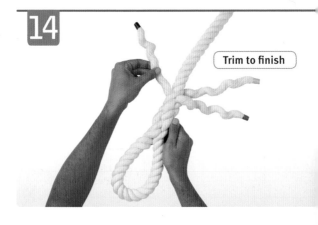

Trim to finish

Short Splice

- A method for permanently joining two ropes of equal thickness.
- Produces a thicker rope.
- May be tapered (see pp.364–69) if desired.
- Use a fid or Swedish fid (see p.19) to make it easier to separate the strands.
- Make three cycles of tucks each way for natural rope and five for synthetic.

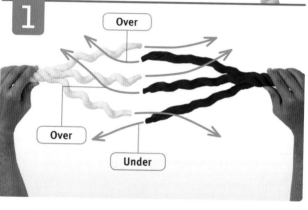

1

Over

Over

Under

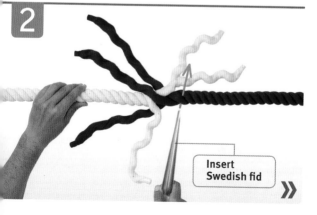

2

Insert Swedish fid

»

3

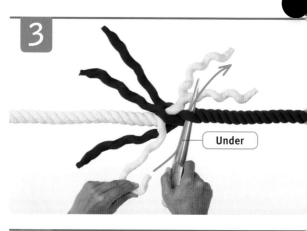

Under

4

Pull

Remove
Swedish fid

5

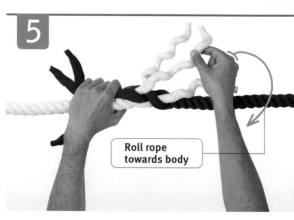

Roll rope
towards body

6

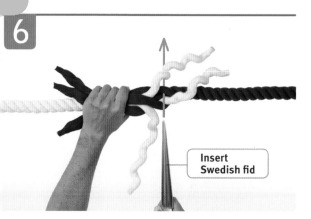

Insert Swedish fid

7

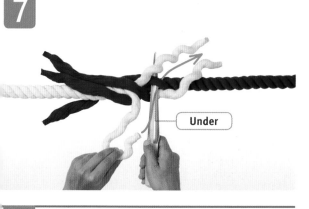

Under

8

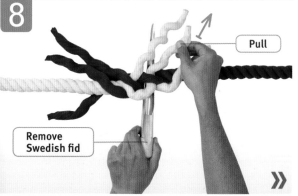

Pull

Remove Swedish fid

》

9

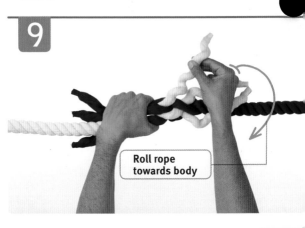

Roll rope towards body

10

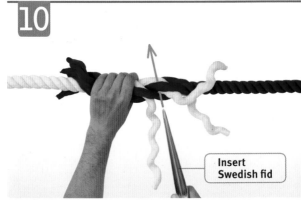

Insert Swedish fid

11

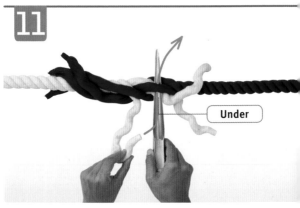

Under

12

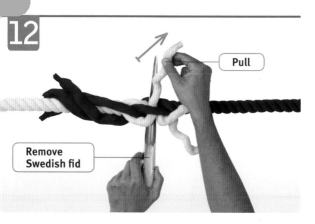

Pull

Remove
Swedish fid

13

Roll rope
towards body

14

Insert
Swedish fid

15

Under

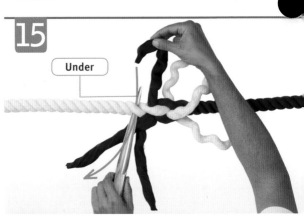

16

Pull

Remove
Swedish fid

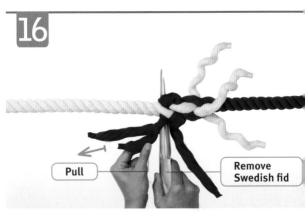

17

Roll rope
towards
body

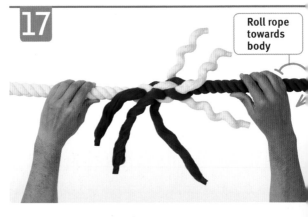

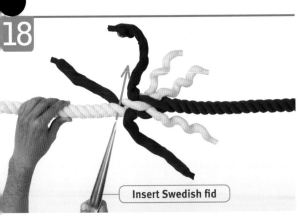

18 Insert Swedish fid

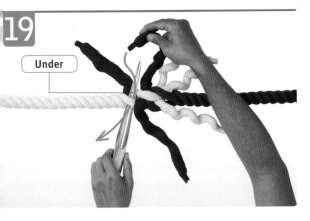

19 Under

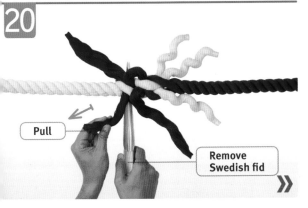

20 Pull Remove Swedish fid

»

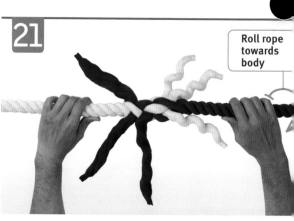

21

Roll rope towards body

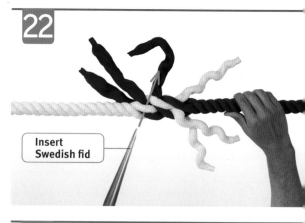

22

Insert Swedish fid

23

Under

24

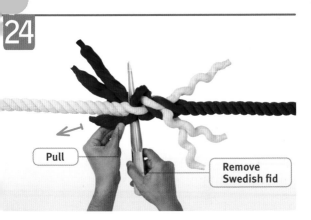

Pull

Remove Swedish fid

25

Begin a second cycle of tucks

Insert Swedish fid

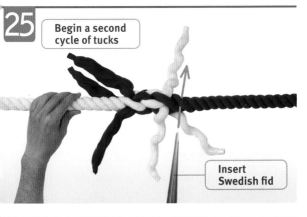

26

Under

»

27

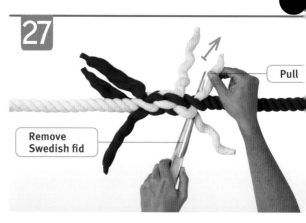

Pull

Remove Swedish fid

28

Roll rope towards body

29

Insert Swedish fid

30

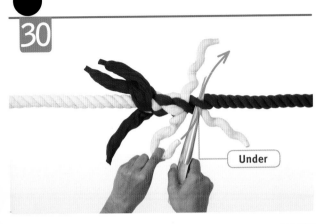

Under

31

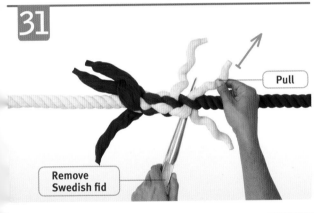

Pull

Remove
Swedish fid

32

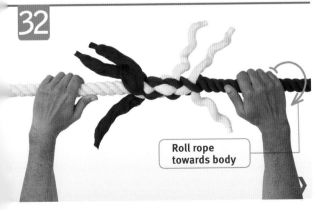

Roll rope
towards body

33

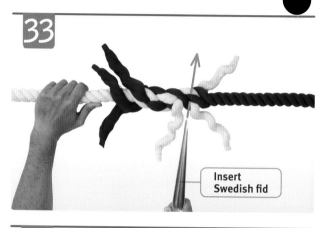

Insert
Swedish fid

34

Under

35

Pull

Remove
Swedish fid

36

Roll rope towards body

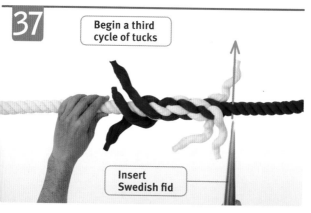

37

Begin a third cycle of tucks

Insert Swedish fid

38

Under

»

39

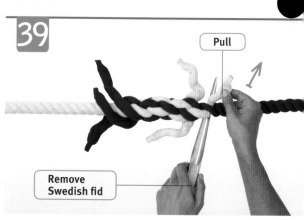

Pull

Remove
Swedish fid

40

Roll rope away
from body

41

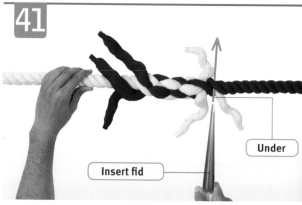

Under

Insert fid

42

Under

43

Pull

44

Roll rope away from body

45

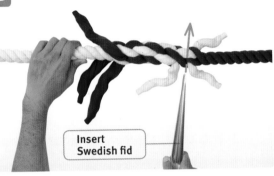

Insert Swedish fid

46

Under

47

Pull

Remove Swedish fid

48

Roll rope away from body

49

Repeat second and third cycle of tucks on the opposite side of the splice

50

Trim to finish

Tapering a Splice

- Used to taper the ends of a spliced (*see pp. 334–63*) three-strand rope to prevent it from working loose.
- Can be used to strengthen and neaten all splices.

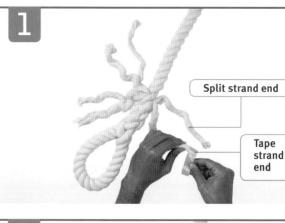

1

Split strand end

Tape strand end

2

Insert Swedish fid

3

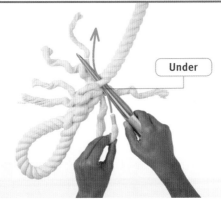

Under

4

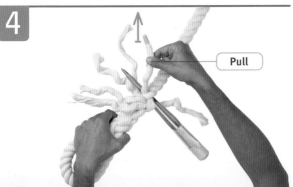

Pull

5

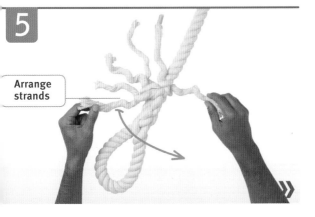

Arrange
strands

»

6

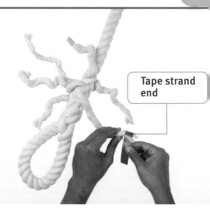

Tape strand end

7

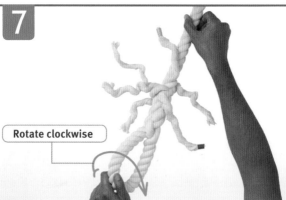

Rotate clockwise

8

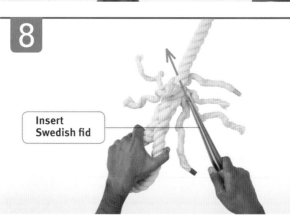

Insert Swedish fid

9

Under

10

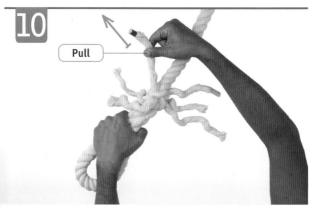

Pull

11

Arrange
strands

»

12

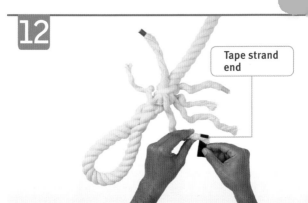

Tape strand end

13

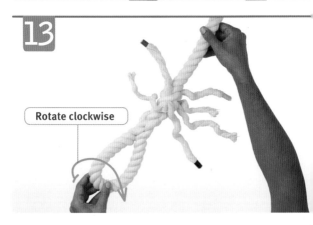

Rotate clockwise

14

Insert Swedish fid

15

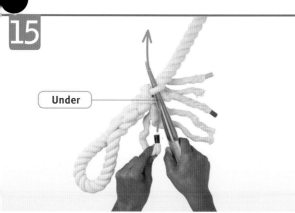

Under

16

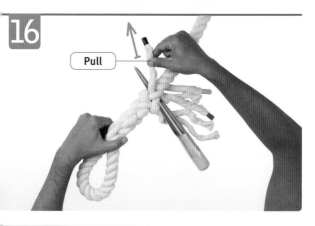

Pull

17

Trim to finish

BEST FOR ...
Horses

Equestrians use knots for a multitude of reasons such as tethering horses safely, fixing clips, tying straps and webbing, and securing ropes around a horse's neck or on the horn of a saddle.

Eye Splice
» pp.342–46

✓ Offers a neat and reliable method for making an eye through which to attach clips to lead ropes.

✓ Should be formed at the end of ropes that are used for pulling, dragging, or hoisting.

✓ Can also be used to make a halter.

Similar knots:
» pp.334–41
Back Splice

Back Splice » p.334–41

✓ Also known as an End Splice, this is a permanent fastening that stops the end of rope from coming undone.

✓ Can also be used to make a grip at the end of a rope.

Similar knots:
» pp.342–46
Eye Splice

Round Turn and Two Half Hitches » pp.180–81

✓ A quick, safe method for tying up a horse – the round turn means it can handle a large amount of strain.

✓ A reasonably easy hitch to untie, even if a large amount of strain has been placed on it.

Similar knots:
**» pp.182–83
Buntline Hitch
» pp.184–85
Fisherman's Bend**

Water Knot » pp.172–73

✓ An effective method for linking flat strapping and webbing of the type found on a horse's bridle.

✓ Can also be used to make an emergency repair to broken reins.

✓ A knot that is both strong and reliable.

Similar knots:
**» pp.157–59
Fisherman's Knot**

Highwayman's Hitch » pp.201–02

✓ A quick-release hitch that is good for temporarily tethering a horse to a ring or rail.

✗ Comes undone easily, so the hitch must always be pulled tight, with a good locking bight, before leaving the horse.

Similar knots:
» pp.180–81
Round Turn and Two Half Hitches

Three-Strand Flat Plait » pp.292–93

✓ Simple and quick to tie, this plait can be made as long as desired.

✓ When secured with a rubber plaiting band it can be used to dress a horse's mane or tail.

✓ A ribbon, held in place with a plaiting band, can be added for extra decoration.

Similar knots:
» pp.294–95 **Four-Strand Flat Plait**
» pp.296–97 **Five-Strand Flat Plait**

Common Whipping

- Prevents the end of a rope from fraying.
- The simplest of all whippings.
- Waxing the twine makes it easier to pull the loop under the whipping turns.
- To finish, use a Marlinespike Hitch (*see pp.199–200*) to prevent fine twine from cutting your fingers.

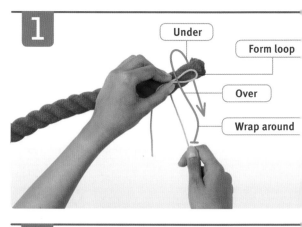

1

- Under
- Form loop
- Over
- Wrap around

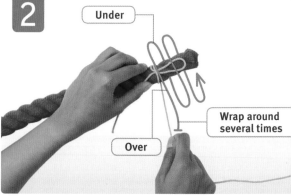

2

- Under
- Over
- Wrap around several times

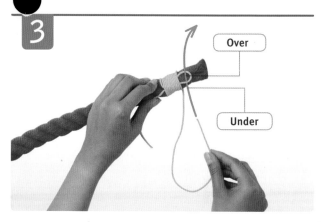

3

Over

Under

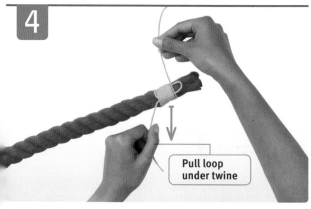

4

Pull loop
under twine

5

Tighten and
trim to finish

French Whipping

- A decorative whipping used to stop a rope end from unravelling.
- Also used over railings or tool handles to provide a firm grip.
- Formed using a series of half hitches (*see p.23*) tied in the same direction.
- Secure the twine around the rope with an Overhand Knot (*see pp.28–29*) before starting.

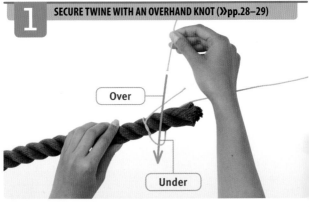

1 SECURE TWINE WITH AN OVERHAND KNOT (**»pp.28–29**)

Over

Under

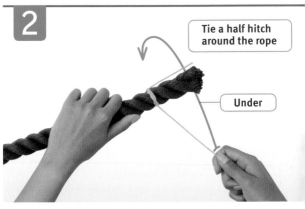

2

Tie a half hitch around the rope

Under

3

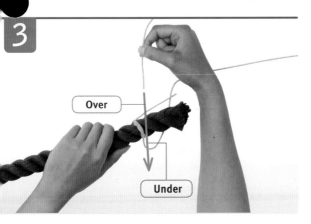

Over

Under

4

Make several more half hitches

Over

Under

Under

Under

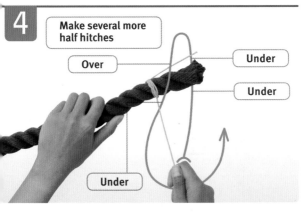

5

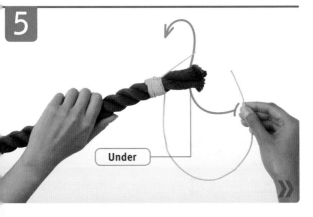

Under

6

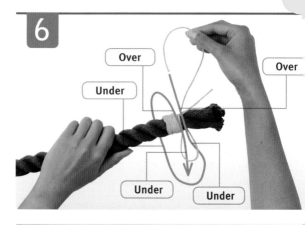

Over

Over

Under

Under

Under

7

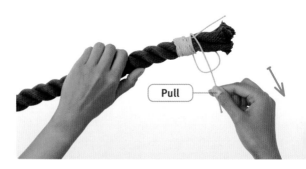

Pull

8

Tighten and trim to finish

Sailmaker's Whipping

The most secure finish for the end of a three-strand rope.

Can only be made at the end of the rope.

Whipping should be roughly one-and-a-half times the diameter of the rope.

1

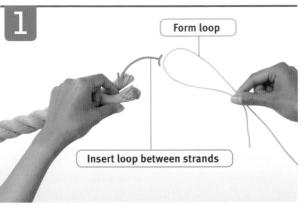

Form loop

Insert loop between strands

2

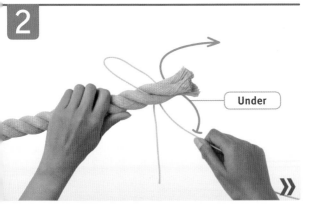

Under

»

3

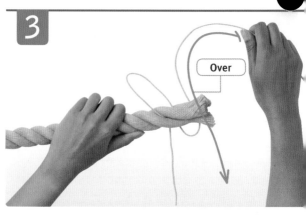

Over

4

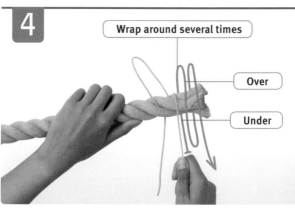

Wrap around several times

Over

Under

5

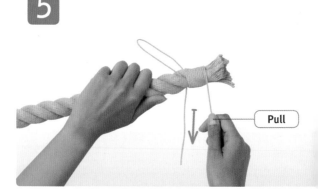

Pull

6

Insert loop between strands

7

Pull

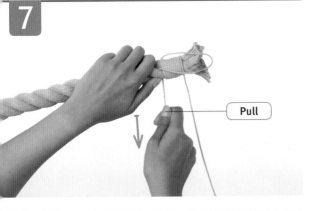

8

Pull to tighten

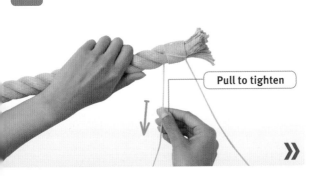

»

9

Insert twine between strands

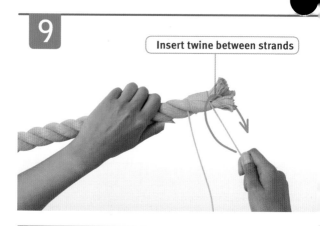

10

Over

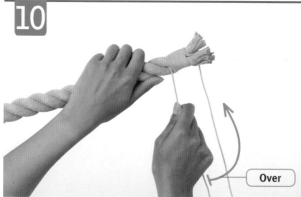

11 FINISH WITH A REEF KNOT (>> pp.85–86)

Palm and Needle Whipping

The perfect whipping to secure a braided rope.

Can be used in the middle of a rope.

Requires a palm and a sailmaker's needle (*see p.19*).

Preferred by sailmakers.

1

Roll rope over as you pull twine through

Through

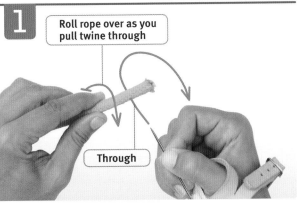

2

Through

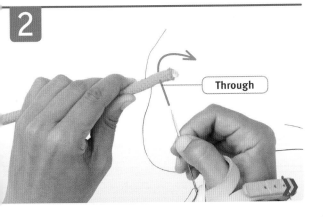

3

Roll rope towards body

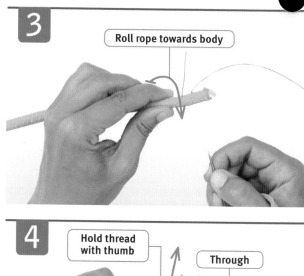

4

Hold thread with thumb

Through

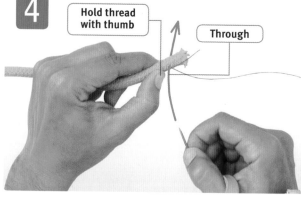

5

Wrap around to cover stitches

Under

Over

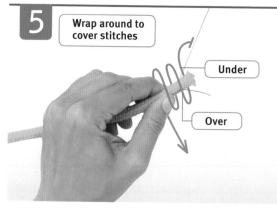

6

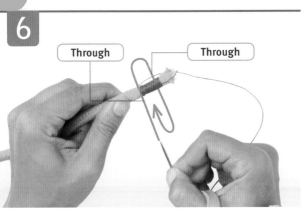

Through

Through

7

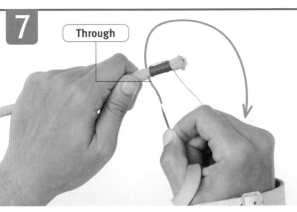

Through

8

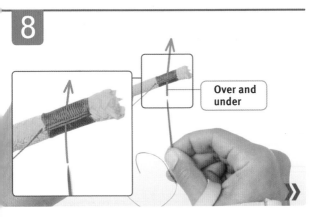

Over and under

»

9

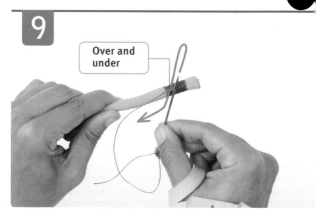

Over and under

10

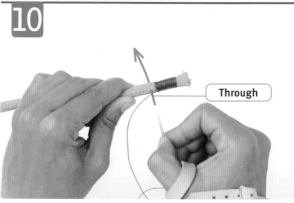

Through

11

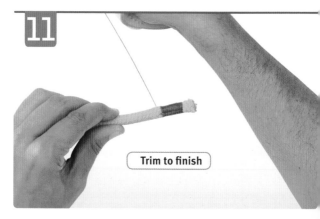

Trim to finish

Seizing

- A tightly compressed whipping that can be used to bind two parts of a rope together.
- Historically used on the heavy fixed rigging found on sailing ships.
- Must be tied tightly and evenly.

1   SECURE TWINE WITH A CONSTRICTOR KNOT (»pp.109–10)

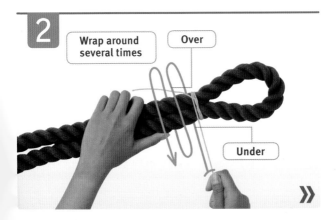

Wrap around

Over

Form loop

Under

2

Wrap around several times

Over

Under

»

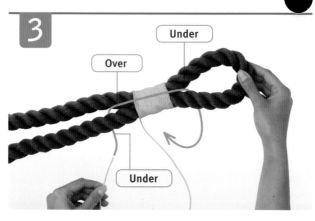

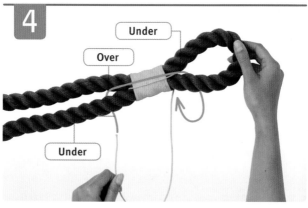

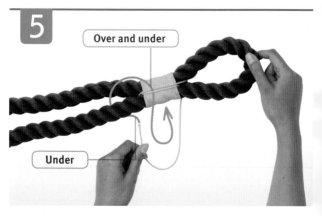

6

Under and over

Over

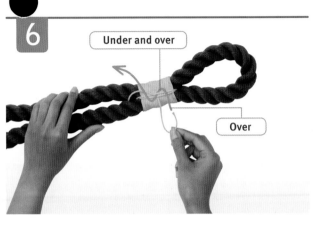

7

Pull to secure

8

Tighten and trim to finish

Stitch and Seize

- Used to make a permanent eye on the end of a braided rope.
- Requires a palm and a sailmaker's needle (*see p.19*).
- Stitch first, then seize over the stitches.
- Make a locking stitch along the seizing halfway through the process for additional security.

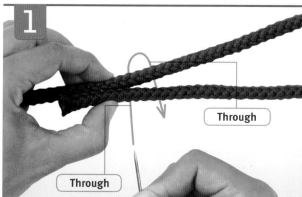

1

Through

Through

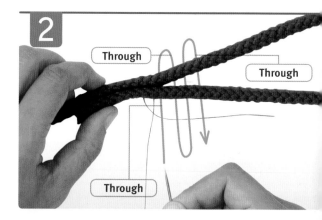

2

Through

Through

Through

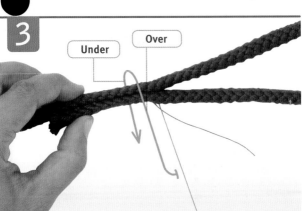

3

Under | Over

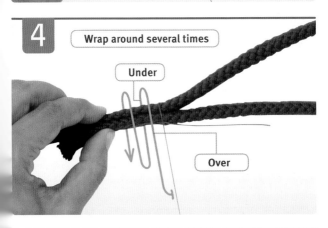

4

Wrap around several times

Under | Over

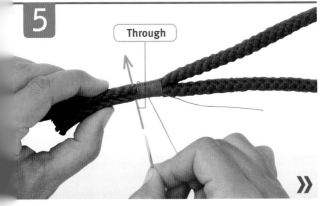

5

Through

»

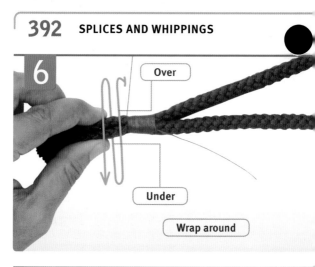

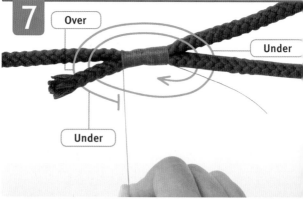

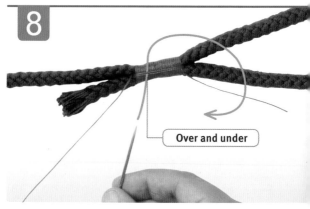

9

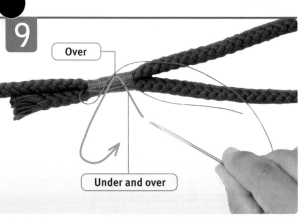

Over

Under and over

10

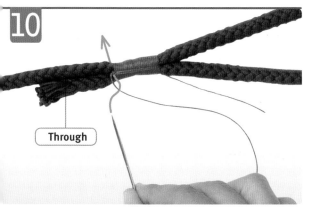

Through

11

Trim to finish

Glossary

As well as explaining the knotting terms used in this book, this glossary also features some specialized climbing and sailing terms.

Belay To secure one climber to another with a rope.

Bight 1 The part of a rope that is folded back on itself to form a narrow loop. **2** The curved side of a knot.

Blood knot Knot consisting of many turns, used in angling or climbing.

Boat hook In sailing, a pole with a hook on one end, used to help catch hold of a rope or ring.

Body The tied part of a knot.

Braid Strands or yarns woven or plaited together in a regular pattern.

Braided rope Rope consisting of multiple woven or plaited strands or yarns.

Breaking rope The part of a rope that controls the amount of slip of a knot, and that restricts the amount of slip a knot has during a fall.

Chafe The frayed part of a rope, caused by abrasion against a rough surface.

Cleat On a boat, a fitting around which a rope is wound to secure it.

Coil A rope that has been placed into a neat series of circles or loops, often for storage purposes.

Cordage The general term for rope.

Core The inner part of a rope which is made from parallel, twisted, or braided rope fibres.

Crossing turn A circle of rope made by crossing one end of a rope over itself.

Eye 1 A hole in a knot. **2** The hole inside a circle of rope. **3** A permanent loop fabricated at the end of a piece of rope. **4** The opening at the end of a fishing hook through which a line can be threaded

Fid A sharp, pointed wooden tool used to separate strands of rope.

Frapping turns Extra turns made across lashing, whipping, or seizing turns.

Half hitch A circle of rope wound around an object or boat fitting. It is kept in place by placing one end of the rope across and at right angles to the other end.

Hard-laid rope Tightly twisted, three-strand rope designed to be very stiff and firm.

Heaving line The light line attached to a mooring rope that is thrown from a boat and used to haul a mooring rope ashore.

Karabiner In climbing, a D-shaped or oval metal snaplink fitted with a locking device.

Laid rope A rope made by twisting strands of yarn together.

Large-diameter rope Rope of around 24mm diameter or more.

Lash; lashing To secure two or more adjacent or crossed poles by binding them with rope; the term for the binding itself.

Lashing turn A turn used to bind poles together, as part of a lashing

ay The direction in which the twists the strands in a laid rope lie.

ead The number of strands used make a plait, used particularly a Turk's Head knot.

ne A length of rope measuring ss than 4mm in diameter.

aded rope The part of a rope that pplies force to a climbing knot.

oop A circle of rope made by acing two parts of a rope together, ithout crossing them over.

arlinespike A slim, pointed, etal spike that is commonly sed to separate strands of rope.

etting needle A pointed tool sed for manipulating fine line hen making a net.

alm A glovelike, leather strap ontaining a metal plate and worn n the hand, to protect the palm hile pushing a sailmaker's needle hrough a rope.

igger Ships' rigging manufacturer.

igging Ropes and spars designed control the sails of a ship.

ound turn A complete circle, llowed by a half circle, made with length of rope around an object.

eize; seizing The process of ining two ropes, or two lengths of rope, by binding them with twine; e term for the binding itself.

heath A covering made from oven strands intended to protect e core of a rope.

heet Rope that controls a sail.

hock cord Rope with a high degree f stretch, made from a rubber astic core covered by a braided rotective sheath of nylon fibres, so known as elasticated cord.

Sling A continuous circle made from rope or tape that can be made by tying the ends of the material with a Fisherman's Knot or a Water Knot. Also referred to as a strop.

Small-diameter rope Rope with a diameter of approximately 4–8mm.

Spade end The flat end of a hook, with no eye for threading line.

Standing part The length of a rope not used or in reserve during the tying of a knot.

Swedish fid A hollow, pointed, metal-bladed tool for tucking strand ends when splicing stiff rope.

Tape In climbing, the flat, woven webbing used to make slings.

Thin line A piece of line measuring less than 2mm in diameter.

Three-strand rope Rope consisting of three strands twisted together.

Tuck To pass one part of a rope underneath another part of itself.

Turn To pass a rope around one side of an object.

Unlaid rope A rope separated into its component strands.

Whipping turn The turn made around the end of a length of rope, as part of a whipping.

Whipping twine A type of thin line, sometimes made from nylon, that is used to bind the end of a rope.

Working end When tying a knot, the end of a rope used.

Working load The maximum load to which a rope should be subjected.

Yarn Natural or synthetic fibres twisted into threads.

Index

Acknowledgments

About the Author
Des Pawson is a global authority on knots who has been producing commercial ropework for over 40 years. He has written several books on the subject of knots and ropework and is a co-founder of the International Guild of Knot Tyers. He has been awarded an MBE for his contribution to the knot and rope industry.
www.despawson.com

Author's Acknowledgments
Putting this book together has been a team effort, not just by the team at DK and at the photographic studio, but by all those people who, over the centuries, have tied knots and shown them to others, so they are still known today. Many thanks to the members, past and present, of the International Guild of Knot Tyers who have stimulated me to develop my knowledge. I have also been lucky in the support and encouragement of my wife Liz who has enabled me to follow my dream as a ropeworker. To all these people, a big thank you.

Publisher's Acknowledgments
Dorling Kindersley would like to thank Gareth Jones, Hugo Wilkinson, and Lee Wilson for their editorial help and Michael Duffy, Phil Gamble, Peter Laws, Hannah Moore, and Yenmai Tsang for their design assistance. Thanks also to Nicholas Brewer for his help with the photography. DK India would like to thank Suchismita Banerjee, Manisha Jain, Tanya Mehrota, Neha Ruth Samuel, and Malavika Talukder.

The publisher would like to thank the following for their kind permission to reproduce their photographs:

(Key: a-above; b-below/bottom; c-centre; f-far; l-left; r-right; t-top)
Alamy Images: fc2 / picturesbyrob 189b; **Corbis**: Bill Holden / cultura 218, Eyecandy Images / Alloy 304b, Roy Morsch / Flirt 276-277b; **Dreamstime.com**: Ildipapp 186; **Getty Images**: Chel Beeson / Photolibrary 302, Jupiterimages / Comstock Images 370, Echo / Cultura 127b, Evan Sklar / Botanica 220-221b, Indeed / Taxi Japan 274, Ascent Xmedia / The Image Bank 166-167b
Jacket images: Front: **Corbis**: Shift Foto
All other images © Dorling Kindersley
For further information see: www.dkimages.com

International Guild of Knot Tyers
If you are interested in learning more about knots and ropework, the International Guild of Knot Tyers (www.igkt.net) offers a wealth of information and resources, and can put you in touch with fellow enthusiasts from the knot-tying community around the world.